Myth and Ritual
in the Plays
of Samuel Beckett

Myth and Ritual in the Plays of Samuel Beckett

EDITED BY
Katherine H. Burkman

Rutherford • Madison • Teaneck
Fairleigh Dickinson University Press
London and Toronto: Associated University Presses

© 1987 by Associated University Presses, Inc.

Associated University Presses
440 Forsgate Drive
Cranbury, NJ 08512

Associated University Presses
25 Sicilian Avenue
London WC1A 2QH, England

Associated University Presses
2133 Royal Windsor Drive
Unit 1
Mississauga, Ontario
Canada L5J 1K5

The paper used in this publication meets the requirements
of the American National Standard for Permanence of Paper
for Printed Library Materials Z39.48-1984.

Library of Congress Cataloging-in-Publication Data

Myth and ritual in the plays of Samuel Beckett.

Includes bibliographies.
1. Beckett, Samuel, 1906–   —Dramatic works.
2. Myth in literature.   3. Ritual in literature.
I. Burkman, Katherine H.
PR6003.E282Z7817   1987   822′.912   86-46026
ISBN 0-8386-3299-8 (alk. paper)

PRINTED IN THE UNITED STATES OF AMERICA

For Emily, Jack, Helen,
and Edgar

Contents

Myth and Demythification

Acknowledgments

I would like to thank all of the contributors to this collection of essays. Their insights, prompt responses, and enthusiasm have made working on the book a great pleasure. I am also grateful to Professor June Schlueter for her perceptive suggestions, to all those at Fairleigh Dickinson University Press and Associated University Presses who have helped the book into print, and to Carolyn South for her help in preparing the manuscript and her moral support.

I also wish to thank the following for their permission to reprint quotations from Samuel Beckett's published and unpublished works:

Faber and Faber Ltd. and Grove Press, Inc. for their permission to quote from *Endgame, Happy Days,* and *Waiting for Godot.*

Samuel Beckett and Henry Ransom Humanities Research Center, The University of Texas at Austin, for permission to quote from Beckett's unpublished Typescript III of "The Way."

Samuel Beckett and The University of Reading Library in England for permission to quote from Beckett's unpublished "Avant Fin de Partie," deposited in the Library's Beckett Archive.

Myth and Ritual
in the Plays
of Samuel Beckett

Myth and Ritual
in the Plays of Samuel Beckett
An Introduction
Katherine H. Burkman

In the barren landscapes of Samuel Beckett's plays, dominated as they are by an ever more encroaching void, one may look in vain for rituals that bring renewal and myths that bespeak a meaningful redemption from that void. Yet Beckett's dramatic world is filled with ritual behavior and is suffused with fragments of old myths. Godot himself, half businessman, half white-bearded Jehovah, would seem to be nothing more than some impotent version of the ever-expected Messiah while the bondage of Didi and Gogo to this offstage figure in *Waiting for Godot* has parodic echoes of the myth of Prometheus. Tempted as one may be to dismiss the kind of obsessive behaviors of Beckett's characters, from the vaudeville routines of *Waiting for Godot* or *Endgame* to the repetitive knocking of Listener in *Ohio Impromptu*, as habit, which as Vladimir says is "a great deadener," one may not do so. For the dynamic of Beckett's plays continuously reveals ways in which habit, as it fails to deaden, takes on a ritual aspect; and ritual in these dramas moves always toward the meanings that linger in the mythical fragments that abound—and even toward the creation of new myths.

On one level, Beckett, like Lucky in his "Think" speech, would seem in his plays to be clinging to fragments of civilization's old truths while he faces the encroaching emptiness, moving too, as Lucky does, to muteness. On another level Beckett's search is more like his Krapp's obsessive spinning of the tapes of his past to find that more personal myth which might somehow give meaning to life and help recover what is lost. The search for meaning is both intensely personal and inward in Beckett's drama, the old myths being no more (or less) useful than Winnie's "Oldstyle," and yet extremely universal, as Beckett seems not only to give the old fragments new life but to move toward the creation of new myths for our time. Speaking of Beckett's tendency in his manuscripts to make his work ever more minimal, Stanley Gontarski remarks, "Beckett's undoing is a means to redress Nietzsche's grievance against what he broadly

13

calls 'Alexandrian culture,' or what we today might call logocentrism: to dispell the myth of causality, to reintroduce ritual elements (through stylized and balletic movement), and to move the drama closer to the spirit of music and away from its mimetic, referential level."[1] Such a demythifying movement is not, however, away from all myth. Even the most secular rites of Beckett's drama continue to connect with mythic themes and sacred rituals that are concerned with the ongoingness of life, the mystery of suffering, death, and rebirth.

Approaches to the definition of myth and ritual and their use in Beckett's plays vary considerably in this collection, ranging from the Jungian to the Marxian to the Lacanian and drawing on the theories of Campbell, Freud, Eliade, Frye, Turner, Girard, Baudrillard, and others. Beneath the variety of approaches, however, the authors share a sense of the complex ways in which myth and ritual operate in the plays as well as a sense of their interconnectedness. There is in the essays an implicit acceptance of the interrelationship of myth and ritual as "symbolical procedures," with myth taken as a "system of word symbols" and ritual as "a system of object and act symbols" that share a "common psychological base." Mythology, in this view, becomes a rationalization of the same human needs that ritual as "an obsessive repetitive activity" dramatizes.[2] What the authors of these essays also share is a sense that Beckett's power as a playwright derives in large measure from a kind of mythic vision that informs his drama.

The emphasis in the first four essays is on the "perilous journeys" that Beckett's more or less immobilized characters manage to take on his stage and the rituals that enable them to cope with and to define their passage. The next two essays explore storytelling in Beckett's plays as means to a ritual rebirth and are followed by three essays that examine various forms of demythification in his drama. The author of the final essay contends that ancient myths still inform the psychology and the structure of the dramas.

Journeying

All of the papers to some extent touch on the quest or journey in Beckett's drama, but four pieces deal particularly with the question of how the characters in the plays manage their journeys. In " 'Getting on': Ritual as Façon in Beckett's Plays," Lois Overbeck examines the way habit, when it becomes invested with significance, works as ritual in such plays as *Endgame, Come and Go,* and an early unpublished fragment, "Avant Fin de Partie." Pointing out the way in which habit becomes rite in these plays, Overbeck notes that habit is not only an evasive tactic used by the characters to deaden their suffering but is also a "façon, a way to get on." The slight changes in the enactment of these habits turn them into ritual in which "pattern makes the connection between past and present possible, but the variants make the pattern significant."

For Susan Brienza in "Perilous Journeys on Beckett's Stages," the business of "getting on" in Beckett's plays, no matter how aimless it seems, still resonates with the ritual and mythic overtones of the archetypal journey of the hero as set forth by Joseph Campbell. Beckett, she claims, "borrows mythic and ritualistic motifs and then parodies, distorts, or transposes them, so that in his plays the arduous path can be simply to the center of a room (in *Endgame*) . . ." or may be temporal, as in Winnie's negotiation of the hours of her day in *Happy Days*. Replacing the trial of killing a dragon with that of getting through the day, the characters, Brienza contends, use the words of their stories as "armor, shield, weapon, and magic potion to be judiciously employed during the perilous quest."

Martha Fehsenfeld in "From the Perspective of an Actress/Critic: Ritual Patterns in Beckett's *Happy Days*" also deals with Winnie's journey through time and her use of habit-ritual as a way of coping. For Fehsenfeld, habit is also an evasive tactic to divert the mind from its suffering. "Pain is constant," she writes, "so in order to accomplish this diversion, one must interrupt its pattern by creating another pattern." For Winnie, ritual becomes a deliberate game in which she is able to achieve a false sense of control.

"No words are necessary to convey the futility of man's passage on this earth," writes Rosette Lamont, in "To Speak the Words of 'The Tribe': The Wordlessness of Samuel Beckett's Metaphysical Clowns." Focusing on three of Beckett's silent pieces, *Act Without Words I, Act Without Words II,* and *Film,* Lamont shows how Beckett moves into the depths of man's unconscious where gesture rather than word defines the nature of Everyman's perilous quest. In these pieces, Beckett's characters become metaphysical clowns as they confront ritual moments of birth and death, enacting ritual routines that allow them to get through their days or seeking in vain to hide from their divided selves.

Storytelling

The focus of Mary Doll's, "Rites of Story: The Old Man at Play" is on those stories that Susan Brienza noted in her piece help the characters through their day. Doll explores the way the narrators of *Endgame, That Time,* and *Ohio Impromptu* "ritualistically *must* tell stories, in order to 'be again' in time." Doll designates three moments in storytelling that make it function as ritual rebirth, not in a traditionally heroic sense but in terms of attaining poetic insight, and she uses Jung's theories of the psyche and Eliade's theory of ritual for her analysis of storytelling as psychic rebirth.

Susan Maughlin, in her "Liminality: An Approach to Artistic Process in *Endgame,*" is particularly concerned with Hamm as creator of his story or chronicle in that play. Using Victor Turner's concept of liminality, Maughlin writes, "It is Turner's premise that cultures set up a dialogue between periods of structure and periods of anti-structure, the later being associated with points of change or transition." Maughlin likens the anti-structure or liminal stage to "the inner workings of the creative process" and offers an analysis of Hamm as artist creating Clov as character both in the play and in the chronicle within the play. "By examining the author/ character metaphor," Maughlin writes, "the components of the 'prolonged creative effort' can be discerned at the height of their strangeness and with all their illogical power."

Myths and Demythification

Stephen Watt is more skeptical about rebirth than Doll or Maughlin in his Marxian discussion of Beckett's characters' forays into Northrop Frye's "green world" in "Beckett by Way of Baudrillard: Toward a Political Reading of Samuel Beckett's Drama." Watt places ritual and myth as "binary opposites" in his paper, defining rituals as those repetitive, formalized actions that tend to conserve social status and structures and myth in terms of Frye's "mythos of spring," the "transforming journeys to forests and enchanted woods which Shakespeare's central characters so routinely take" and Victor Turner's concepts of liminality, anti-structure, and *communitas.* For Watt, the plays are essentially failed rites in which characters such as Hamm in *Endgame* may yearn for the anti-structure and *communitas* of the green world but tend to prefer their world of objects and the "maintenance of a fetishized consumption." Beckett's characters cling to objects, Watt asserts, "whose real nature is less attractive than their signifying value." The temporary verbal flights to the green world (mythmaking), Watt contends, only serve to reinvest the values of the society from which the characters choose never really to depart.

What Watt suggests, then, is a failure on the part of Beckett's characters to achieve myth or inhabit the green world about which they dream or tell. Claudia Clausius in "Bad Habits While Waiting for Godot: The Demythification of Ritual," and Phyllis Carey, in "The Ritual of Human Techné in *Happy Days,*" both comment less on a retreat from myth to a kind of negative, conservative ritual than they do on Beckett's tendency to demythify.

Clausius's emphasis is on the use of parodied ritual for purposes of demythification. "Our habits and rituals," she writes, "are undressed, laid bare, exposed, so to speak, when Beckett demonstrates both their most basic function—to pass the time—as well as their ultimate failure to achieve this satisfactorily." In Chaplinesque fashion, the tramps play with the conventions of social life, "deflating the value of convention" and engaging the audience in their humanity at the same time that they reveal to them the absurdity of their shared situation. The demythification for Clausius is not finally negative, for habit may be a "great deadener," "but habit parodied quickens us to new insights, even within the limitation of yet another ritual, the theater."

Sharing Stephen Watt's dark view of the self-imprisoning rituals of a materialistic culture that he finds in Beckett's plays, Phyllis Carey writes, "What *Happy Days* drama'tizes on one level is a world seen from a technological perspective, a mental construct to which humans have continually adapted themselves until they seem to be merely playing out the last stages of a self-destructive ritual." The myths of "the old style" and the bits of her classics that Winnie calls forth fail her and are demythified along with the rituals that call them forth.

Carey, however, shares Clausius's view that Beckett shapes an aesthetic ritual that takes us beyond the failure of those enacted in the plays. Winnie's storytelling, as opposed to her calling up of her classics, conjures up an "inner myth," Carey suggests, one that "focuses on origins, the fall from innocence, human vulnerability." Winnie's scream, at the climax of her story, prepares us for a moment of recognition in the silent look between Winnie and Willie at play's end—a recognition that is at the heart of effective ritual. "Opposed to the deterministic entropy and impotent hermetic attempts at transformation within the play," Carey writes, "is the aesthetic shaping of the drama itself to provide the viewer a moment of participation in the silence and the stare, an artistic shaping of ritual to enable a transformation of human vision."

In the final piece in the book, "A Blink in the Mirror: From Oedipus to Narcissus and Back in the Drama of Samuel Beckett," Judith Roof explores Beckett's use of the myths of Oedipus and Narcissus that she contends underlie the psychology (Lacanian) and structure of his plays. Roof sees the shift from Beckett's pairs of characters in some of his early plays to his triangles in *Play, Come and Go,* and *Catastrophe,* as "both an expansion and reduction of Beckett's dramatic universe," one that allows him to put a "different emphasis on an enigmatic narcissistic mirror which remains at the end of the plays as reduction and regression from an Oedipal past."

When contemplating the characters in *Play* as struggling like Sisyphus rather than progressing, Roof reminds us of Camus's mythic vision of an absurd hero rising in some way above his situation. The authors in this book differ on the question of whether Beckett's characters enjoy any victories of the Camus variety just as they differ on their views of how myth and ritual operate in the plays. But as they explore some of the

Katherine H. Burkman

"perilous journeys on Beckett's stages," in terms of myth and ritual, they provide us with important new landmarks that help illumine the experience of the plays.

Notes

1. S. E. Gontarski, *The Intent of Undoing in Samuel Beckett's Dramatic Texts* (Bloomington: Indiana University Press, 1985), p. 184.

2. Clyde Kluckhohn, "Myth and Ritual: A General Theory," in *Myth and Literature: Contemporary Theory and Practice,* ed. John B. Vickery, pp. 39, 44. In this essay Kluckhohn discusses the debate over the theory that myths are verbalizations of rituals as something of a chicken-and-egg question. He is more concerned to show that ritual, on the level of behavior or action, and myth, on the verbal level, answer to the same needs of people seeking some form of control over their experience and their world. "Rituals and myths supply, then, fixed points," writes the anthropologist, "in a world of bewildering change and disappointment" (p. 43).

JOURNEYING

"Getting On"
Ritual as Façon in Beckett's Plays
Lois More Overbeck

Winnie *(Happy Days)* has her bag of props and the bell. Hamm *(Endgame)* has his storytelling ("Then babble, babble, words, like the solitary child who turns himself into children, two, three, so as to be together and whisper together, in the dark") and his place in the center.[1] In *Footfalls,* May paces. Habit is a way "by which man functionally relates to time," says Beckett in *Proust;* it "empties the mystery of its threat."[2] As a façon de vivre ("way of life"), habit approaches ritual when it is invested with significance, when its "comforting illusion" of control invests the self with meaning.[3] In "Ulysses, Order and Myth," T. S. Eliot suggests that myth "is a way of controlling, of ordering, of giving shape and a significance to the immense panorama of futility and anarchy which is contemporary history."[4] Eliot believes in this possibility, whereas ritual patterns in Beckett's work seem to expose the futility in tension with the persistent desire of the human spirit to make it other.

In his essay *On Humor,* Pirandello comments on the human tendency to "fix what is changeable and fluid . . . to give absolute value to what is relative"; and he adds that "man is given . . . the privilege of feeling himself alive with the fine illusion that this inner feeling really exists outside of himself."[5] The illusion is enticing. Beckett's Unnamable reflects: "I invented it all . . . [to] allow me to think of myself as somewhere on a road moving between a beginning and an end," but he concludes, "All lies."[6]

In an early unpublished fragment, "Avant Fin de Partie," Hamm's prototype, X, describes his situation. He says that he is both "aveugle et paralyse" ("blind and paralyzed"), yet he also says "En réalité je vois assez clair et je marcherais bien . . ." ("In reality I see clearly enough and I could walk well").[7] The paradoxes of seeing though blind, of moving on through life while paralyzed, intrigue. On one level, X, like Hamm, has his factotum, F/Clov, to fulfill physically the functions of sight and movement. In another sense, X manages to "go on" because routine and habit are part of his way. X describes his "façon de vivre": "Comme c'est bon méditer à haute voix, surtout le matin, avant que se dechaîne le train-train quotidien" ("How good it is to contemplate aloud, especially in the morning, before breaking into the daily routine") (p. 1). He continues, "Cela fait partie de ma vie, cela fait partie de ma rountine" ("This is/makes part of my life, this is/makes part of my routine") (p. 1). Here *partie* suggests "to belong to," meaning that it forms part of a pattern. It is in this sense of making a pattern ("fait partie de ma vie . . . fait partie de ma routine"), of the habit ("train-train quotidien"), and of the notion that things are taking their course (en train), that this way (façon) approaches ritual.

However, the title of the play, *Fin de Partie,* also suggests a game, that is, a temporary ordering of reality. In "Avant Fin de Partie," X does not confer meaning on or derive meaning from his façon: "Je ne represente rien, ne signifie rien que je sache" ("I represent nothing, signify nothing, that I know") and "Ce qui se passe ice ne signifie rien seulement que je sache" ("What happens here signifies nothing only that I know") (p. 1). The qualifying phrase "que je sache" allows for doubt, but X does not harbor illusions about his actions. By contrast, Hamm has glimpses into self-awareness but prefers to make his façon de vivre into ritual because without it he would be alone with his fear. In "Avant Fin de Partie," X projects his routine onto others, calling upon F to dress for one role after another; yet he himself refuses the identity of master. In *Endgame,* Hamm pursues storytelling and through it narratively projects multiple roles for himself. Hamm knows them as his façon (i.e. "We're not beginning to . . . to mean something?"), but he also flirts with the temptation to make them real. He imagines that a rational being might observe them and under-stand: "And without going so far as that, we ourselves . . . *(with emotion)* . . . we ourselves . . . at certain moments . . . *(vehemently).* To think perhaps it won't all have been for nothing" (pp. 32–33).

By way of reply, Clov has a flea. Clov takes a long view of time; he has suffered enough: "Finished, it's finished, nearly finished, it must be nearly finished" (p. 1). He is the active partner in the "train-train quotidien" ("the daily routine"): the inspections at the windows, the ashbins, his uncovering of Hamm. He refuses to cover Hamm up again because he has "things to do." Although he can play the verbal game, for Clov "All life long [is] the same questions, the same answers" (p. 5). Clov is a realist about time: "Grain upon grain, one by one, and one day suddenly, there's a heap, a little heap, the impossible heap" (p. 1).

Hamm, on the other hand is eager for "divertisement"; he says, "Ah the old questions, the old answers, there's nothing like them!" (p. 38).[8] Hamm takes comfort in the pattern. In *Proust,* Beckett notes that "the creature of habit turns aside from the object that cannot be made to correspond with his . . . team of syntheses" (pp. 11–12). This seems to be Hamm's reaction throughout *Endgame.* Each time that Clov says "I'll leave you," Hamm ignores the threat by initiating another gambit; he asks an old question and expects an old answer.

CLOV: . . . I have things to do.
         (Pause.)
HAMM: Did you ever see my eyes?

                                                          (P. 3)

CLOV: I'll leave you, I have things to do.
HAMM: Do you remember when you came here?

                                                          (P. 37)

CLOV: I'll leave you.
HAMM: Is my dog ready?

                                                          (P. 39)

CLOV: I'll leave you.
HAMM: Have you had your visions?

                                                          (P. 41)

Although both think that "this has gone on long enough," even such self-conscious observation is a part of their routine. Hamm concludes, "Then it's a day like any other day" whereas Clov comments, "All life long the same inanities" (p. 45). The difference in their attitudes toward routine and toward time is evident in the gesture of the alarm clock. Clov thinks that the end is "terrific"; Hamm prefers the "middle" (p. 48). Hamm's is always "the life to come." Although the nullity of existence intrudes despite his façon, Hamm prefers the "train-train" to the ending. If something is "taking its course," this holds out the hope of some meaning, which is better than nothing.

Hamm needs constantly to reassure himself that he really exists outside of himself. He must be in the center; he needs coordinates to define himself. His façon allows him to go on: "Perhaps I could go on with my story, end it and begin another" (p. 69). He can project an ending for himself, but it is in the future perfect tense: "I'll have called my father . . ." (p. 69). He knows, "If I can hold my peace, and sit quietly, it will all be over with sound and motion, all over and done with" (p. 69), but he cannot be still. Hamm tries on the possibility that "I was never there. . . . Absent, always, it all happened without me. I don't know what's happened," but Clov undercuts this rationalization: "What for Christ's sake does it matter?" (p. 75).

When his façon runs down like the clock, when there is no more painkiller and the anesthesia of ritual gambits no longer hides the heap that does not add up to a life, when Clov no longer answers his call, Hamm glimpses himself as ending—"Moments for nothing, now as always, time was never and time is over, reckoning closed and story ended" (p. 83). However, even in ending, Hamm can only play with an image of nonbeing: before covering his face with the handkerchief, he addresses it as "old stancher" and makes it into a collaborator. He would like to believe in the ritual and would like the ritual to define him so that he can evade the possibility that what is human may be only a "tiny flash in . . . the cosmic dark."9

In *Endgame,* repetitive routines, gambits, storytelling—all offer a sense of time that is circular rather than linear. Although only diversion, such repetition suggests rebeginning, as does ritual. Yet even in ritual, repetition is only virtual. While act and re-enactment may be nearly exact, both exist within the linear dimensions of time. No moment can ever be the same as it has been before. Repetition in drama poses a similar doubleness: action and the echo of previous enactment are both simultaneous and discontinuous in repetition. Within dramatic convention, we may be convinced that the repeated act is really the same as before: characters invest it with solemnity, as if doing it again for the first time. However, the very repetition which suggests identity also points to the impossibility of identity: thus repetition, even in ritual, is a measure of time as a continuum. Certainly this is the case in Beckett's dramaticule, *Come and Go.*

In *Come and Go,* pattern repeats in permutations, but, as X suggests in "Avant Fin de Partie", "C'est toujours la même chose, mais les termes changent, il me semble, un peu, du jour au lendemain, surlendemain" ("It is always the same thing, but the terms change, it seems to me, a little, from one day to the next, to the next") (p. 2). Stage movement is choreographed to suggest that each woman walks her own circular path in the shadow, and yet the journey for each is the same, just as we infer that the secrets repeated in ritual patterns are similar—shadows of mortality.

With hats brimming their faces, long coats covering their feet, the three women of *Come and Go,* companions of childhood, sit together on a bench surrounded by darkness. Together they speak only briefly about their common memory of sitting on a log in the yard at Miss Wade's school; this conversation is uneasy smalltalk in the moments of ensemble, the intervals between the going and coming. Each of the three, in turn, leaves the lighted center (Beckett specified that they are to move effortlessly and merge with the shadows—no sound of footsteps, no visible feet). With choreography suggestive of the sleight-of-hand artist (button under the thimble), when the center figures leaves, the one on the left slides over to whisper a secret to the figure on the right; when the first returns, she takes the open position on the left. After a moment of recollections about their shared childhood, the figure seated in the center leaves, and the one on the right slides over to whisper a secret into the ear of the figure on the left, and so on. The pattern repeats in full permutation.

When each in turn has gone and come, and they are again together on the bench (with positions inverted), each knows a secret about the others, and the others know a secret about her. Though none can tell, all of the secrets are the same (each has been shared in virtually identical language and gesture); the secret is the mortality embodied by the title *(Come and Go)*. This mortality is also embodied in the images of the play.

For lack of a possible conversation about the present or the future, the women retreat to a stylized gesture of the past and link their hands in the "old way" (echo of *Happy Days,* it suggests a place when time had significance). The figure on the right holds the left hands of each of the others; the one on the left holds both right hands, the one in the center holds a right and a left. Flo says, "I can feel the rings,"[10] although Beckett's stage directions indicate that they wear no rings. The ritual gesture of clasped hands allows them to keep their secrets from each other, but the image of feeling the rings evokes the cycle of time. Twice turned upon itself, the bond of the three women (forever linked in their untold secrets) is never again what it was, never again what it seems to be. Something is the same, and everything is different.

Joined together as they are, their gesture suggests a Möbius strip—"a length of paper, twisted once, the two ends of which are pasted together, thus forming a surface that has neither front nor back," beginning nor ending.[11] The Möbius strip is a three dimensional shape resembling the sign for infinity (∞); it is both linear and circular. Its double loop is such that if an ant were to crawl along its surface, it would return to its beginning point but on the other side. The "invention" of the Unnamable and the façon of Hamm are linear: "somewhere on a road moving between a beginning and an end" (p. 414). The imagery of *Come and Go* suggests that time is a cycle turning again and again on itself, like an hourglass. The ritual gesture of clasped hands is an attempt to deny the terror of mortality in which life is "come and gone in no time gone in no time" *(That Time).*[12] At the same time, the ritual gesture dramatizes the feelings the three women attempt to evade. In *Come and Go,* the soft circle of light reveals the edges of darkness.

The image of infinity, a figure eight turned on its side, has been noted in Beckett's dramaturgy by Enoch Brater, who cites Beckett's commentary on Denis Devlin in *Transition* and applies the image to May's movement in *Footfalls.*[13] May's pacing, wheel, and turn is perceived along a horizontal plane as "movement from right to left, from left to right," says Brater; but from above "we would see the tracing on the stage floor of a tremendously elongated variation of the figure 8 turned on its side . . . the mathematical symbol for infinity."[14]

In a 1981 unpublished typescript, tentatively entitled "The Way," the infinity sign recurs, first as a figure eight and then placed horizontally.[15] Here is the Beckettian journey through time distilled: "The way wound up from foot to top and thence on another way." There is "no retracing," only going on—although there is freedom "to pause or not" at the "foot and top." The way is taken apace, a steady gait so predictably "a foot a second or mile an hour and more" that distance could be calculated from the time, if time could be "numbered." The way is one of thorns, mist, half-light, and "loose sand underfoot." It winds and turns and continues on, tracing a path that suggests the pace, wheel, and pace of May in *Footfalls*. The steadiness of the journey and its direction again suggest the image of an hourglass with its flow of sand.

Placed horizontally, the figure eight suggests infinity. Although this allusion would suggest a contrast, the way continues "Forth and back across a barren same winding one-way way." The sun is still and the shadows are long "before and after." The way loops apace with no measure of time or distance; there is "Bedrock underfoot" but the ends are "groundless." The way is trod; indeed the trodding seems to define it: "Through the emptiness the beaten ways as fixed as if enclosed." The context makes the way seem finite, for beyond it is "unending void. In unending ending or beginning light."

Yet in both the vertical and horizontal axes of "The Way" the movement described is continuous and fluid, save for the pauses possible at the extremities. Neither piece comes to closure, although the last lines of each are the same: "So no sign of remains a sign that none before. No one ever before so—" Even here, in the distillation of the Beckettian way, ritual repetition seeks significance, seeks a sign of others as a sign of self, but finds "were the eye to look unending void."

John R. Daniel suggests that "ritual emptied of meaning" is farce; but that is not what we see in these plays.[16] On the other hand, neither do we see that ritual in itself is capable of transforming reality. Nonetheless, ritual as used in these plays provides a compelling image. By allowing us to see ritual as a means of evading the reality of the void, as a means of seeking meaning in the void, Beckett's work seems to expose the futility of such goals in tension with the desire to reach them. Because of this ability to express the tension, ritual enacted in art may empower compassion for and by the human spirit. Beckett's art may be the "remains" which say, to me at least, another *has* come before.

Notes

1. Samuel Beckett, *Endgame* (New York: Grove Press, 1958), p. 70. All subsequent references to *Endgame* are to this edition.

2. Samuel Beckett, *Proust* (New York: Grove Press, 1970), pp. 7–8, 11. All subsequent references to *Proust* are to this edition.

3. Ruby Cohn, *Just Play: Beckett's Theater* (Princeton: Princeton University Press, 1980), p. 12. Translations in the text are my own.

4. T. S. Eliot, "Ulysses, Order, and Myth," *The Dial*, 75 (1923): 483.

5. Luigi Pirandello, *On Humor,* trans. Antonio Illiano and Daniel P. Testa, *North Carolina Studies in Comparative Literature,* 58 (Chapel Hill: University of North Carolina Press, 1974), pp. 140, xiii.

6. Samuel Beckett, *The Unnamable* in *Three Novels: Molloy, Malone Dies,*

The Unnamable (New York: Grove Press, 1955), p. 414. All subsequent references to *The Unnamable* are from this edition.

7. Samuel Beckett, an untitled typescript held in Reading University Library and marked "Avant Fin de Partie." It is described as A under *Fin de Partie* by Richard L. Admussen, *The Samuel Beckett Manuscripts* (Boston: G. K. Hall & Co., 1979), p. 50. With permission of Samuel Beckett and the University of Reading Archives. Citation is from p. 1. All subsequent references from "Avant Fin de Partie" are from this typescript.

8. Dina Sherzer, "Beckett's *Endgame,* or What Talk Can Do," *Modern Drama,* 22 (1979): 295.

9. D. C. Muecke, *The Compass of Irony* (London: Methuen and Co., 1969), p. 151.

10. Samuel Beckett, *Come and Go* in *Cascando and other Short Dramatic Pieces* (New York: Grove Press, 1964), p. 69.

11. Kobo Abe, *Woman in the Dunes,* trans. E. Dale Saunders (New York: Random House, 1964), p. 99.

12. Samuel Beckett, *That Time* in *Ends and Odds: Eight New Dramatic Pieces* (New York: Grove Press, 1976), p. 37.

13. Enoch Brater, "A Footnote to Footfalls: Footsteps of Infinity on Beckett's Narrow Space," *Comparative Drama,* 12 (Spring 1978): 37. Brater cites Samuel Beckett, "Dennis Devlin," *Transition,* 27 (1938): 292.

14. Enoch Brater, "Still/Beckett: The Essential and the Incidental," *Journal of Modern Literature,* 6 (February 1977): 6.

15. Samuel Beckett, "The Way," ["provisional title"], an unpublished typescript dated 1981. With permission of Samuel Beckett and The Humanities Research Center, Austin, Texas. Quotations are taken from no. 434, Typescript III, "which is a carbon copy and without markings" suggesting "the presence, elsewhere, of the ribbon copy of Typescript III, with, very likely, additional revisions by the author." *No Symbols Where None Intended: A Catalogue of Books, Manuscripts, and Other Material Relating to Samuel Beckett in the Collections of the Humanities Research Center, Selected and Described by Carlton Lake* (Austin: The Humanities Research Center, 1984), pp. 172–73. All subsequent quotations from "The Way" are from this Typescript, which is one page long.

16. John R. Daniel, "Ionesco and the Ritual of Nihilism," *Drama Survey,* 1 (May 1961): 63.

Perilous Journeys on Beckett's Stages

Traveling through Words

Susan D. Brienza

A hero's difficult journey to a home, an enchanted center, or a sacred place, accompanied by near-impossible tasks and trials, has been an archetype of myth and literature for centuries. Samuel Beckett early in his career demonstrated an interest in and an understanding of myth generally, and of archetypal figures particularly, in his article about Joyce's use of Vico;[1] and we know from his biography that he read some Jung. Thus he had ample background to allow him to play freely with the mythic frame of the journey and turn it to his own dramatic ends.[2] Elements of the wandering-hero pattern include a summons, rough terrain filled with obstacles, the crossing of a threshold, helpers who aid the hero with knowledge or with magic, a passage through some sort of dark underworld, often a pilgrimage to a religious center, and eventual completion of a successful mission. For his drama, Beckett borrows mythic and ritualistic elements from several sources and then parodies, distorts, or transposes them; for example, while there is a long tradition of the travel theme in Noh drama and in primitive trance plays, in Beckett's theater physical travel becomes minimal and often goal-less. He uses the quest motif as a frame for a different sort of journey, with parallels not to physical action on stage but to psychological searches, metaphysical struggles, and linguistic voyages.

Traditionally the journeying hero searches for some new knowledge of self, or is tested in order to earn new status; but his true identity is rarely in doubt. In the middle of the voyage, according to many myths, the hero may temporarily lose or hide his real name; he may also lose companions, ship, clothes, and even genital organs—all links to the waking world—in order to prepare him for the twilight or threshold world from which he will eventually emerge. For Beckett's wandering fragments of men, however, limbs are lost, never to be regained, and characters enter the dark zone with no hope of an exit. In a pilgrimage or rite of passage a wanderer

28

would begin at a familiar place, journey to "a Far Place" where communication occurs through "the telling of recondite origin-myths or other kinds of gnomic utterances, secret languages," and then return to the familiar place, being changed in some way[3] but Beckett's creatures often find themselves quite literally stuck in the Far Place. The pilgrim submits to his ordeals because his penance is a voluntary act, chosen in hopes of a miraculous transformation;[4] by contrast, Beckett characters suffer a penance they have not chosen, and no redemptive miracles occur. During their painful journeys, Beckett heroes in both the plays and the novels are halted or stymied by various handicaps, usually lameness or blindness,[5] their destination unknown or unaccomplished. It seems ludicrous for an author to apply the wandering-hero motif to characters who can scarcely move, yet this is what Beckett does. He appropriates journey motifs and then subverts them or inverts them ironically, thus heightening both the tragedy and the comedy of his drama. For Beckett's perilous linguistic and creative journeys on the stage, language plays all the parts: antagonist, helper, obstacle, goal, vehicle.

Simply examining a few of the stage plays in chronological order demonstrates the regression from physical activity to stasis. In *Waiting for Godot* Pozzo and Lucky are seen in the middle of a long journey to a fair in act 1, but act 2 finds their pace slowed because of Pozzo's blindness and their now-hazy goal. The tramps are of course the most mobile of Beckett's protagonists, yet they feel somehow "tied" to Godot and therefore to a particular place.[6] When they say "Let's go" at the end, the audience knows that they could (and in a rational world, should) continue their quest for meaning elsewhere, but of course they do not move. *Endgame* also concludes in tableau with Clov, who has been announcing and threatening his departure throughout the play to the seated and lame Hamm. Clov at the end of his game, poised on the brink of leaving, is all dressed up (he now has changed from house slippers to hiking boots and has a hat, jacket, and suitcase) with no place to go. Krapp can walk back to his pantry periodically to sneak a drink, but after each short trip he seems compelled to return to his desk and sit hunched over his tape recorder; he is psychologically rather than physically frozen, and yet mentally he traverses great distances back to the past. In *Happy Days* Winnie, of course, is rooted to a particular spot *in* the earth and by act 2 suffers immobilization of head and arms as well as legs, so that she can move only eyes. Her mind, though, is racing as she runs through fields of language.

For many of his characters Beckett retains minimal, usually repetitive, physical movement, but this is not necessarily the journey that interests the audience or the myth-seeker. On the surface the arduous path may be simply to the center of a room (in *Endgame*), or ostensibly to a mundane train station (in the radio play *All That Fall*). On a deeper level, however, in

Beckett's rites of theater (and in his later fiction) when the heroes become more infirm, more fixed, they begin to travel within the mind itself, as perilous journeys increasingly shift from the external to the internal; this has become one constant in his world. Then words become not just a magic formula for entry, as they would in the wanderer myth, but the totality of the voyage: vehicle, companion; helper, goal.

                              *   *   *

   The Beckett hero as mythic traveler is more directly visible in the fiction than in the drama, most prominently in *Molloy* where explicit references to people and events from the pages of the Bible, Homer, Virgil, and Dante abound. In Beckett's plays the travel myth instead appears allusively, as undertone and as resonance rather than as surface reference. Yet however faint and parodied, the journey myth is still present in paradigm. After glancing at some mythic patterns in his fiction, we can begin to see the framework for how Beckett interweaves similar material—with more indirection and subtlety—in the drama.
   In *Molloy,* the protagonist's journey, first toward an alter ego and then toward the mother lode of Self, is hampered by archetypal obstacles and ordeals[7] that compose the entire plot of the novel. Besides assuming parodic qualities of Lord Ragland's hero, Sir James Frazer's gods, and Otto Rank's well-born heroes, Molloy becomes Beckett's particular prototype—the traveler as writer. (Ruby Cohn has nicknamed Beckett's wandering narrators "walk-talkers.") Molloy is an author who, as Rubin Rabinovitz reminds us, works in a strange verb tense, what the narrator calls "the mythological present"; thus it is not surprising that Molloy tries on several different mythic roles including the "spiritual voyager" and "the intellectual adventurer, mental traveller, or wandering scholar."[8] His pilgrimage takes him through forest and city, but we perceive—even if he does not—that he is going out in order to go in, that his voyage truly begins only when he rests and writes in his mother's bed. In the next novel, Malone writing in his own bed tries to center himself within stories drawn from the circumference of the external world, but, since he then searches inward rather then outward for company and material, he is constantly shifting and decentering, and finally imagines that he is inside another's head.[9] Gradually "inside" and "outside" lose all meaning—since in the following novel the Unnamable is continuously in the same predicament, as he begins and ends by seeking a *place* in which to exist—and Malone abandons all hope for a centered identity.
   After Molloy has reached an origin, then Malone, the Unnamable, and the "I" of *Texts for Nothing* are less successful with the quest for the self; and here Ludovic Janvier's distinction for the fiction between place of narration and narration of place helps us see that while protagonist/ narrators are fixed in rooms, beds, bottles, or mud, their created alter egos

are free to wander through elaborate circles and spirals.[10] What Janvier neglects, however, is that in the next set of fictions geometrical structures of both setting and narrative stance, although still based on the mythic circle, become much more complex. In *How It Is* the narrator tries to place and thus to find himself among imagined millions in an infinite set of ordered pairs arranged along an infinite number line, which he keeps proclaiming is "not circular" although the structure of the novel obviously *is*. In *Imagination Dead Imagine* the place of narration is superimposed on the narration of place, both meeting in a rotunda within a white dome (a construction that unmistakably represents a skull—"rap, solid throughout, the ring as in the imagination the ring of bone") with two bodies, bent at right angles, disposed around the *center* of the inner circle. For *The Lost Ones* Beckett fabricates a cylinder with physical niches and mazes suggesting mental convolutions. When this story was dramatized as a monologue, the speaker addressed the audience as one with the creatures roaming the "abode," included them as "searchers" for a "way out," and thereby made the theater itself a mental microcosm like the "closed space" of the cylinder. This recent production and the later plays convince Beckett readers beyond all structural doubts that the boundaries between genres are blurring and breaking; especially in the last fifteen years, Beckett's plays contain extended stories or are reducible to monologues, the fictions favor dramatic and cinematic techniques, and both forms achieve a lyricism of language and a litany of prose rhythms akin to poetry. Thus it is simplistic to divide fiction and drama neatly and then to say of Beckett's theater, as Janvier does, that "here are the safety rails and limits" where Beckett "stabilizes his creatures," beings who are "[n]o longer focused on the self."[11] Instead, Beckett's stage protagonists are wandering in the same psychological circles and suffering the same creative pains as all those Merciers and Molloys.

In the midst of writing the trilogy of novels begun with *Molloy*—fictions that concern an agonizing search for the Self (the ideal core of the onion Beckett envisioned in *Proust*) and which pushed its author painfully and relentlessly into his own self, Beckett turned, for relief (!), to the writing of *Waiting for Godot*—a play that also uses various myths as intellectual (and perhaps personal) anchors. *Godot* is a ritualistic drama that takes the notion of the wanderer hero and shrinks it—comically yet tragically—to almost nothing. Instead of a quest for a Holy Grail, a pilgrimage to a Mecca, or even a vigil for a messiah, we witness the results of a journey to an unfamiliar place, at an unknowable time, to meet a pseudo-savior of uncertain name, for an unstated purpose. From the very beginning, then, Beckett has exploited the quest motif—but for his own ironic purposes— in these dramatic journeys to nowhere. And especially for *Godot* and *Endgame*, which are highly self-reflexive and metatheatrical, the only possible encounter takes place between the actors, the search is for more dialogue, and the perilous journey is through the play itself—through language, and through real and stage time (which often for Beckett's theater is measured by the same clock).

The voyage becomes no easier when it is temporal rather than spatial: Winnie, already located in the center of her mound in *Happy Days,* must somehow navigate the hours between the bell for waking and the bell for sleeping. Frequently on Beckett's stage, whether his characters are waiting, sitting, crawling, or walking, the trial is not to reach a magic forest, to kill a dragon or to win a maiden, but merely to get through the day, one more station for Everyman's Way of the Cross. Time as well as space must be physically traversed in Beckett's universe,[12] his world consisting of "vast tracts of time," a phrase from the novel *How It Is* that also describes the geography of the plays. And for his drama as well as his fiction, the means of passing the time is storytelling or just plain talking; thus words become armor, shield, weapon, and magic potion to be judiciously employed during the perilous and paradoxical quest. After all other actions and objects are stripped away, language remains the only companion during life's journey—with special force and poignancy in the recently dramatized short story, *Company.* In effect, words become not just the primary means of travel, but also an end of travel: maintaining a continuous flow of language to evade a horror *or* determining the precise formulation of words that will allow one to go silent is the main goal of the intellectual and spiritual journey.

*   *   *

Beckett's use and abuse of the stage provides insight into his ironic and parodic development of the wanderer motif. Stage space, after the tree and road in *Godot,* moves with some exceptions from outdoors to indoors, and then to a mental landscape. Although *Endgame*'s set consists of a room, it represents the artificial playing area of a chessboard; even more abstract, its two windows looking out on the earth turn the stage into a giant skull (as critical consensus decided and as Beckett has confirmed when he directs the play), and Hamm himself speaks repeatedly of something dripping in his head. The fact that word journeys are tortuous is demonstrated by Hamm's bleeding face and Veronica's veil (several of Beckett's heroes are Christ-like in their suffering, their artistic crucifixions). And his phrase "It's finished," the savior's reported last words on the cross, prompts us to remember where Christ was crucified: at a cranium-shaped place called "Golgotha" or "Calvary" which derive from words meaning, respectively, place of the skull and upper dome of the skull.[13] In a recent playlet, *A Piece of Monologue,* there is a prop that Beckett describes in the stage directions as "standard lamp, skull-sized white globe, faintly lit"; an artificial skull glows next to the dying speaker's actual head on stage.

Winnie's bleak and blazing landscape, a hell of the mind, is—one hopes—not of this world, certainly not naturalistic and not permitting travel other than intellectual. In *Play* the locale shifts to the purgatory of three post-mortem souls with heads stuck in urns centered on stage; for the three actors, then, their container *is* their stage. The radio plays, in totally abolishing a physical performing area, internalize all action and dialogue; and *Embers,* as an extreme extension of the conventions of the genre itself, plays solely inside Henry's head. Beckett's television drama *Eh, Joe* uses the camera to peer into the brain as its perspective gradually deepens from Joe in his room to a close-up of Joe's face, to a framing of his tortured eyes, all the while a female voice-over transcribing the protagonist's thoughts. In the later stage play *That Time* we see against a totally dark backdrop only an ancient man's head on a pillow, facing us portrait-like ten feet above stage level, as three voices coming from beyond the stage recall disjointed eras of the man's life.

Further disembodied and fragmented is the protagonist in *Not I,* Mouth: in this minimalization, merely a pair of exaggerated lips with tongue and teeth. A mouth floating high above the stage (in fact flouting the normal human dimensions of the playing space and denying the existence of the stage floor) gives the audience the eerie impression that they too are inside a head, the giant theater cavern surrounding Mouth. Both secular and religious rituals can provide parallels for such off-center use of a performance arena: Victor Turner notes that initiands must go *outside* social structures to locate their new selves, and that often Christian pilgrimage destinations would be located at "peripheral places," for example, on the outskirts of a city.[14] A religious structure, a church, is specifically foregrounded at the end of a later play, *Footfalls.* May recalls a time when she began to leave home to pace: "Slip out at nightfall and into the little church by the north door, always locked at that hour, and walk, up and down, up and down, his poor arm" (p. 242). Literally she is walking along the "arms" of a cross-shaped church; figuratively she is searching for an inner self, a real identity, as she listens to evidence of her corporeal presence and hugs her own arms closely about herself. May, who later declares "I was not there" in church and who at the end of the play suddenly vanishes, takes her place in the long tradition of wanderers who pass through a threshold to accomplish self-annihilation:

> . . . the hero goes inward, to be born again. The disappearance corresponds to the passing of a worshipper into a temple—where he is to be quickened by the recollection of who and what he is, namely dust and ashes unless immortal. The temple interior, the belly of the whale, and the heavenly land beyond, above, and below the confines of the world, are one and the same.[15]

But May cannot die—and therefore can never be reborn—because she was never fully alive: Beckett has said during rehearsals that for this character he had in mind Jung's lecture about a girl who did not actually experience birth, and thus only "existed," didn't "live."[16] Hence May's footfalls continue: "when as though she had never been, it never been, she began to walk."

While it is apparently true that throughout *Footfalls* May is pacing on realistic floorboards, presumably in a room in a house, her mother's words, "Will you never have done revolving it all?" extend physical space to a mental area. Although the question refers to May's revolving and wheeling path across the floor, it includes cognitive rotations when the mother in her next speech adds "[revolving it] In your poor mind" (p. 240). Thus Beckett's stage shrinks to a platform for interior journeys and then expands to subsume or to suggest a huge skull where the word journey continues. (Once more the fiction is explicit where the drama is allusively implicit; in a recent story called "For to End Yet Again" Beckett depicts a scene that is similar to his recent stage spaces: ". . . skull alone in the dark the void no neck no face just the box last place of all in the dark the void." And the narrator of *Ill Seen Ill Said,* published in 1983, confirms that we are "in the madhouse of the skull and nowhere else.")

In the dramatic, skull-like settings with characters becoming increasingly static, each minimal prop and tiny action takes on enormous impact and import as Beckett focuses on the journey of a hand or the opening of an eye. Thus Pierre Chabert accurately argues that "immobilization of the body, the elimination of all movement in space, as in *Happy Days,* or of all gestures, as in *Play,* reduces the actor and the stage to words alone," and insures that "both word and gesture are restored to a primal expressive function."[17] Aware of this ritualistic function, we can trace exactly how and why stasis paradoxically turns into activity on Beckett's stage. What the audience is watching, besides the diminutive alterations of eyelid flickerings or slight curls of the fingers (tiny quivers magnified in huge spaces) is the motion of a mind at work—the twists and turns of the imagination and the swift manipulation of language, all for the re-creation of past selves and the projection of future ones. Using the vision of imagination, we witness a wandering through a mental terrain, a consciousness trying desperately to reach the goal of an identity or at least the certainty of existence. This explains why, for example, the dramatization of *Company,* an hour and ten minute monologue by a seated protagonist, grips an audience forcefully and seems not static but varied and strangely dynamic.

* * *

Oddly enough, Beckett's first radio play, *All That Fall,* contains his most realistic setting: rural roads and country noises. On the surface the entire play consists of a physical journey to a train station and back home, and every segment of the trip is frustrating and slow, with the sound of "dragging feet" permeating the background. From the start, the donkey stymied with old age and stubbornness stands for Mrs. Rooney and her halting progress: "But a moment ago she neighed and pawed the ground. And now she refuses to advance. Give her a good welt on the rump. . . . Well! If someone were to do that for me I should not dally" (p. 13). But it matters not whether one rests or moves, for stasis or travel can be equally dangerous, as Maddy Rooney herself maintains: "It is suicide to be abroad. But what is it to be at home, Mr. Tyler, what is it to be at home? A lingering dissolution" (p. 15). During the trainward journey, besides various tests and trials, Maddy also encounters what are known in the mythological paradigm as "helpers," agents who befriend her, aid her, propel her along. With every element of the journey archetype, however, Beckett can be playfully ironic; here the helper is a man with the unfortunate name of "Slocum" whose vehicle breaks down as soon as he helps Maddy into it. Despite these dubious aids (human, not supernatural, in Beckett's world) Maddy complains of the misery she endured travelling; the return home is even more arduous because now she must lead her blind spouse (she becomes *his* helper). For his part, the only joy he can derive from the walk is a secular and sterile ritual, the patterning of arithmetic that has lent an illusion of order to many a Beckett character; for him, counting the steps is "One of the few satisfactions in life!" Conversely, what he dreads most is "stopping and starting again," particularly when Maddy would suddenly "stop dead," because then inertia reigns and he must help transport her 200 pounds.

Throughout the play physical movement and verbal agility are linked, subtly at the beginning when Mrs. Rooney's lines about Mr. Slocum's car describe the progress of the play as well: "Start her up, I beseech you, and let us be off. This is awful!" (p. 18). Similar speeches in *Waiting for Godot* and *Endgame* self-consciously comment on the nonaction of those plays as if the drama itself is a goal-less wanderer or vehicle moving too slowly. Husband and wife in *All That Fall* have opposing attitudes to the relation between walking and talking, Mr. Rooney complaining "Once and for all, do not ask me to speak and move at the same time" (p. 29), whereas Mrs. Rooney battles with her native tongue just as she wrestles with locomotion. After she expresses hope for a "safe haven," her husband notes that "sometimes one would think you are struggling with a dead language" (p. 34). But her prose is very much alive with dual meanings when her answer to Dan's "Where was I in my composition?" is the playfully double "At a standstill." Mr. Rooney appreciates neither her attempts at creative communication nor her need for physical communion. The body of English language, the physical body, and mechanical bodies, all fall—and all fall short.

Endless huffing, puffing, and shuffling during their painfully retarded journey is even more effective aurally on the invisible stage—since this drama was written for radio—than it would be on the visible one. All these slow and somber steps lead only to the grave; it may be Mr. Rooney's birthday, but for the small boy fallen or pushed under the tracks it is a funeral day. When Maddy mourns the lateness of the hour and the misfit in society offers to consult her watch, Mr. Tyler remarks, "We all know, Miss Fitt, we all know only too well what the time is now getting on for" . . . (p. 26). In fact, to all the characters tramping in the dust of life's road, the mortal dust stirred up never to settle, Maddy warns that death is the only real terminus:

MR SLOCUM: May I offer you a lift, Mrs Rooney? Are you going in my
            direction?
MRS ROONEY: I am, Mr Slocum, we all are. . . .

(P. 17)

We are indeed all going in the direction of sickness and mortality, the universality of the road shown here in its historical progression of vehicles from primitive cart to modern train; and we are all on a quest for salvation and transcendence, a journey that in Beckett's world is usually frustrated and ultimately futile.[18]

Although one critic terms *All That Fall* "an anti-fertility ritual" because of its apparent celebration of sterility,[19] another perspective sees the ending of the play as elevated to a positive statement. From this point of view, Maddy could actually rejuvenate language and bring tangible human warmth to this sterile place: "as a "[m]onument to creativity," Maddy, "artistlike, creates a world of words"; the wind at the end of the play becomes her symbol of energy and life, converging to a union and a rising up of the Rooneys at the conclusion, and thus effecting an actual birth day—not necessarily a celebration of Mr. Rooney's birth but of the renaissance of language.[20] Yet even though this focus on Maddy does result in a more optimistic interpretation, the reading rings a few false notes considering the overwhelming sorrow of this drama littered with dead and dying, and orchestrated with the mournful song "Death and the Maiden" in the background. Perhaps the body of language, if not the human one, can be ressurrected (words, like messiahs, will "come again," as Winnie says in *Happy Days*); perhaps the theater can be an arena for ritual renewal even if the actual world is damned. The overall tone of the play suggests a ritual preparation for the journey toward death and the encounter with the void, a ritual movement that could evoke at least a sense of calm, as in the Tibetan *Book of the Dead*.

Just as the cosmos of *All That Fall* is diseased, dying, or dead, the world beyond the stage in *Endgame* is "Corpsed," and "outside of here it's death." Although character speeches and gestures are formal and cere-monial, particularly in their rituals of beginnings and endings, these rites become comic parodies; "the play mocks rather than affirms 'order.'"[21] We have a regal figure, an ironic kind of harvest god, in Hamm, but he cannot walk; and Clov, the only mobile character, has presumably reached the end of life's larger voyage with his habitation in the shelter. The short journeys possible to him now—like a trapped knight reduced to stalling maneuvers on a chessboard, as critics have noted—are the finite, futile treks back and forth between Hamm's room and the kitchen, varied only by the trips up and down the ladder to peer out the two windows at the back of the stage. Clov's ascensions of the ladder are ritualistically signifi-cant, though, because in several cultures, and as depicted in many dif-ferent art forms, a ladder serves as the road from earth to heaven (for instance, Jacob's ladder up to God in the Old Testament). Ironically here, however, the voyage upward leads to no paradise; on the other side of his walls, the periphery of a hellish existence, is, Hamm warns, the "other hell" (pp. 25–26). Thus Clov's examinations of the outside world from the top of the ladder elicit a bitter "brief laugh." Since no physical place can now provide a worthy goal for a quest, and since the current shelter promises only a false, deceptive "refuge," the characters in *Endgame* transport themselves in their imaginations—for example, Nell and Nagg traveling back to happy and romantic moments on Lake Como with their memories and enjoying the ritual retelling of the tailor story about Crea-tion. Hamm daily continues his verbal progress through his "chronicle" as he dreams of travel, of physical escape (pp. 34–35). And the story itself is described in terms of movement, as if it were an endless journey: Hamm admits that he is able to "get on" with it but "not very far, you know, not very far" (p. 59). Even the saying of a prayer, beseeching God for some kind of solace, metaphorically becomes a procession of mental motion as both Hamm and Clov initiate their praying with the phrase "Off we go."

Paradoxically fixed in his chair yet mobile when Clov wheels the seated deity about, kingly and domineering Hamm wants to command what little universe remains and thus terms his circular orbit of the Shelter's periph-ery "Right round the world!" He demands to feel the wall with his hand as Clov takes him on the voyage—as if he is surveying in a tactile manner (because he cannot do so visually) his entire domain. Then, his central place in the room must be regained just as the center must be located for a ritual ceremony or by a quester being tried; and yet his precise spot in the middle continuously eludes him. Besides the analogy to a chess player struggling to control the middle of the board, in a mysteriously ritualistic way Hamm's striving for the center is linked to his preoccupation with order and power, since his shelter suggests a microcosm of the mythologi-cal Universal Round: "the continuance of the cosmic order is assured only by a controlled flow of power from the source."[22] In psychological terms, to be "centered" means to be in control of oneself and thus have the power of stability—a security that the fragmented Unnamable utterly lacks and that all Beckett's characters vainly seek. Hamm, the ham actor as well as insecure psyche, needs to be the center of attention, wants his parents constantly listening and his dog continuously looking at him. Beckett, too, desired to maintain order when he directed the play in Berlin in 1967; calling the geometric precision and patterning he sought "Pythagorean," he stipulated that Hamm's chair be at the absolute center, that Hamm's position at the end be identical to that at the start, and—most meticulously—wanted the three characters when praying to form equilateral triangles with their hands and heads.[23]

Clov tries to establish absolute order within his kitchen (of equal dimensions) and his pantry (with regulated provisions), yet Hamm vacillates between demanding accurate placement and settling for an approximate situation:

CLOV: We haven't done the round.
HAMM: Back to my place!
       (Clov pushes chair back to center.)
       Is that my place?
CLOV: Yes, that's your place.
HAMM: Am I right in the center?
CLOV: I'll measure it.
HAMM: More or less! More or less!
CLOV: *(Moving chair slightly):* There!
HAMM: I'm more or less in the center?
CLOV: I'd say so.
HAMM: You'd say so! Put me right in the center!
CLOV: I'll go and get the tape.
HAMM: Roughly! Roughly!
       (Clov moves chair slightly.)
       Bang in the center!
CLOV: There!
       (Pause.)
HAMM: I feel a little too far to the left.
       (Clov moves chair slightly.)
       Now I feel a little too far to the right.
       (Clov moves chair slightly.)
       I feel a little too far forward.
       (Clov moves chair slightly.)
       Now I feel a little too far back.
       (Clov moves chair slightly.)

(Pp. 26–27)

This fastidiousness over the exact center provides him with what he fundamentally seeks—more interaction and converse with Clov. Minute by minute what keeps both Hamm and Clov there—there together and there on stage—is, as they admit, "the dialogue," the old questions and the old answers in ritualistic repetition, that is, the interchange of more words.

The main function of the more extended "linguistic creation," the continuing story, is to forge a mythic past that will allow them to project or extrapolate a "mythical present"; thus Hamm and Clov attempt to win control in a fluctuating, decentered world by mythologizing through the cumulative creation of a "Chronicle" carrying the connotations of history.[24] In yet another way, Hamm's day-by-day Chronicle gives purpose to his life as each segment of the story brings him closer to, yet farther from, the saga's conclusion. And words themselves as Clov's master and Hamm's teaser, become personified: Words drive them on, Words keep trying to mean something.[25] Paradoxically, language in *Endgame* plays the role both of obstacle and of helper.

During the languishing toward the end of time, Hamm and Clov notice how many items are running out: biscuits, bicycles, painkiller, even coffins; and Winnie too frets that she has "come to the end of [her] own resources" (p. 27). But in *Happy Days* the prized commodities become words themselves. She waits for the right moment of the day to raise her parasol, to open her bag, and to perform her song (which serve as obsessive rituals for her); most important, though, she is worried not just that she will lack objects or activities but that language—whether in the old style or the new—will abandon her:

> . . . What now? *(Pause.)* Words fail, there are times when even they fail. . . . What is one to do then, until they come again? (P. 24)

It is as if syllables compose Zeno's tiny grains of sand in an hourglass, and all the linguistic granules will fall faster than the earth will revolve. Winnie repeats the image for infinite duration that Hamm had also used ("the millet grains of . . . that old Greek"), and in act 1 with her large bosom and wide earth skirt she herself resembles a huge hourglass. Besides feeling that she must not deplete too quickly her words allotted for the day, she fears that language is the only vehicle she *can* employ to journey through time, which is certainly true after the objects in her bag are no longer available diversions in act 2. Since words reliably fill time, Winnie is even more inventive with word games than the *Godot* tramps—and of course her trial of waiting is infinitely more static.

In order to keep the words going, Winnie exploits many linguistic and rhetorical ploys, developing more creativity in proportion to her panic. For longer passages she has ready at hand many set pieces—her prayer, her song, the anecdote about Mr. Shower, and the story about Mildred— all of which she resorts to at least twice. At the sentence level she multiplies words by repeating her need for Willie as witness (at least 8 times) and by reiterating sentence openers that imply she has created her own proverbs, her own standard phrases: "that is what I always say" in act 1, which is shortened to "I say" in act 2. She is "saying" in a vacuum since Willie seldom answers; but her solution for this is to carry on what may be called a rhetorical dialogue with him, anticipating his responses, sometimes stating his supposed answer and then replying to that, for example, "I think you would back me up there, Willie" (p. 31). Yet unlike the archetypal agent or helper, Willie rarely aids Winnie in continuing her verbal journey. Forced, therefore, to be independently creative, in fact playing the playwright for a few segments, Winnie supplies actual lines for Willie: "Oh I can well imagine what is passing through your mind, it is not enough to have to listen to the woman, now I must look at her as well" (p. 29). Adding culture and verve to her running commentary about the day, Winnie's classical quotations, even though distorted and distilled, do renew and replenish language and enable her to hold up prose as a shield, another "sunshade," against reality and time.

As words run out, though, one augmenting device of Winnie is simply to permute them, as the Unnamable and Watt had learned: "There is so little one can say, one says it all. *(Pause.)* All one can" (p. 51). At the morphological level she can fill up the space of her day with semantic quibbles, reminicent of the self-conscious prose of the protagonist of *Texts for Nothing,* as she repeatedly questions the meaning of "hog," "day," and "life": "Yes, life I suppose, there is no other word" (p. 28). With the word "hair," even when she knows she has the correct term, Winnie vacillates over its grammatical category thus generating more sentences to speak; is it singular or plural, "it" or "them"? (pp. 22–23). And on each occasion that the problematic word "day" appears Winnie automatically adds "to speak in the old style," since time itself, an eternal blazing sun, no longer moves her through a finite unit of existence. Like the wanderer or quester who is required to utter precisely the correct words in precisely the correct order as an effective formula, Winnie seems to fear disaster if she fails in her exact performance of linguistic ritual.

In the following passage the impending dearth of language is termed a "danger," one of the trials of Winnie's static, metaphorical quest; and three consecutive times words to *say* are given precedence as desirable resources over things to *do:*

Ah yes, so little to say, so little to do, and the fear so great, certain days, of finding oneself . . . left, with hours still to run, before the bell for sleep, and nothing more to say, nothing more to do, that the days go by, certain days go by, quite by, the bell goes, and little or nothing said, little or nothing done. *(Raising parasol.)* That is the danger. *(Turning front.)*

To be guarded against. *(She gazes front, holding up parasol with right hand. Maximum pause.)* (P. 35)

A pause of great length signals anxiety of maximum intensity for Winnie. There is an interesting parallel with Noh drama here: the highest emotional level calls forth the least physical movement, a near stillness of performers. Some say that "the soul is dancing" during this time, that nine-tenths of the minimal motion represents a dance of spirit while only one-tenth is the dance of the body.[26] Of course in Beckett's ironic transposition, this moment of suspension signals terror, not jubilation or transcendence.

Winnie hysterically denies that she has become so desperate that she must talk to herself, and significantly she always depicts this hypothetical state of speaking a monologue *sans* auditor as being lost in the "wilderness," being a traveler in uncharted territory, the great bog of the unknowable soul. Ironically, she is, of course, rambling to herself throughout most of the play—sometimes even thinking aloud about her actions and possessions the way lone children at play might do. With linguistic miles to go before she sleeps, and with certain activities and objects too early and easy a rescue, Winnie must create other verbal aids; and at two points she solves the predicament of loneliness and endless time by taking the gun from her purse and transforming it into a character: she addresses Brownie with exasperation. "No, not you again." In act 1 she can rummage through her bag and in a sense travel across her face as she examines it and applies make-up,[27] but with her arms buried in act 2, words provide, quite literally, the only gestures, and metaphorically the only movement. Structurally words do begin to desert her, since act 2 is half the length of act 1 and contains about half as many literary allusions. When she feels impossibly stalled in speech, she asks herself, "And now?" and later prods herself forward with the imperative, "On, Winnie." For the quester venturing through stage time, words are supremely important because, finally, they become company on the road, the only helpers, and more fundamentally, the only indication of the travelers' existence, and thus the primary weapon against solitude.

In the radio play *Embers* (1959), roughly concurrent with the original French version of *Happy Days,* the first two spoken words refer to progress in both walking and talking when Henry simultaneously pushes his boots and his mind "On. [stage directions] On!" (p. 95). As he strolls the shore his main quest is to force an answer about life's meaning and suicide's motivation from his drowned father's spirit, just as Winnie's goal is to entice a reply from Willie. Obviously, the goal is never attained, and both Henry's father and Winnie's husband refuse to perform the function of aiding agent, Willie's few replies being woefully inadequate and his approach at the end being ambiguous at best. Once again Words must come to the rescue to replace all nonhelpers, and language will at least move the journey through time. When talking to his wife, Ada, Henry literally conjoins physical and verbal travel with a variant of the first phrase "on" as he angrily responds to Ada's pause with: "Drive on, drive on! Why do people always stop in the middle of what they are saying?" (p. 116). The next time he prompts Ada's dialogue forward, he links linguistic and temporal units just as Winnie had done when she sifted through her grains of sand in a day: "Keep on, keep on! *(Imploringly.)* Keep it going, Ada, every syllable is a second gained" (p. 117). Uttered syllables also serve to drown the incessant sound of the sea in Henry's ears.

Theatre II, a "rough" written around 1960, has one character, A, blatantly state what Beckett's stage people have been doing since *Godot:* "Let us kill the time here, talking of this and that." If words can be marshalled against time, they can also be used by A and B to determine the true nature, the real self, of C as they read through—"at top speed"—a report about him. Throughout the dialogue between A and B runs the idea of a narrative journey, with admonitions to "Keep going, keep going" and prods like "Come on, we're getting nowhere, get on with it" (pp. 92, 95). Again employing the travel metaphor, they end their review of the biographical report as if it were the goal of a voyage: "It's heavy going, but we're nearly home" (p. 95).

The notion of going faster in order to travel literarily across a space of time is exploited in a radio play two years later, *Cascando.* Here Voice and Music are prompted by Opener, who begins by setting the drama in the month of May, a ritual period of renewal, and who in mid-play emphasizes the time: "Yes, correct, the month of May. /You know, the reawakening" (p. 141). Yet in this artistic wasteland "dry as dust" there is no rejuvenation possible. While Opener speaks of time, Voice concentrates on space, imagining fictional settings and focusing on spatial metaphors.[28] Whenever Music and Voice sound together, they express that common Beckettian need to get "on" with a story through phrases like "on . . . getting on . . . finish," "to the end . . . come on," "we're there . . . nearly," in which it becomes clear that the story's end is depicted as the goal of a journey. Plainly the identification of verbal progress with motion is embedded in the English language, but Beckett by design literalizes and foregrounds this ambiguity. Opener continues the spatial metaphor: "We have not much further to go" (p. 141), and Voice speaking alone is most explicit about physical travel: "—no tiller . . . no thwarts . . . no oars . . . afloat," then "—faster . . . out . . . driving out . . . rearing . . . plunging . . . heading nowhere." At the end, Voice and Music are working together, anxiously striving to get somewhere: "we're there . . . nearly

. . . . just a few more [words]," and finally they conclude on the road again where most Beckett characters also start; "on . . .
come on . . . come on—" (p. 144). With a flow of language punctuated
with ellipses and a symbolic pattern of acquatic travel (tillers, oars
"afloat"), Beckett teases us with the Christian symbolism of water as
purification and the classical Oriental concept of the river of time. But his
monologues with ironic ritual echoes can swell to floods of words rushing
out of control, streams that will just as soon engulf as baptize you, as soon
drown as float you.

For later dramas, the protagonist is less driven and driving because he is
more alone—haunted by vague voices and feeling as much a listener as a
speaker. There dwells little "communitas," that spirit of fellowship and
community generated by the ordeals of pilgrimages or initiatory trials
during a liminal state; this state of intellectual thresholds and social
marginality can include all drama, but especially applies to ritual drama,
and particularly to Beckett's ritualistic drama.[29] In *Godot* the tramps feel
the communitas of mutual dependence and of real affection; in *Endgame* a
certain loyalty and liking persists even during a battle for power, and all
four prisoners of the shelter must endure together—Nag suffering the end
of the sugar plums, and Hamm suffering the lack of an ending. Most
clearly, in *All That Fall* the travelers share the communitas that arises from
hard times on the road. Denying all human community, *Company,* a 1980
Beckett short story recently dramatized by the author, ends with the word
"alone": a lone man lying in the dark tells lies, fictions, devising other
voices to keep himself company.

When *Company*'s figure was still capable of motion he had walked the
equivalent of several circuits around the earth's equator by embarking on
circular paths within a one-mile radius of his home (p. 60). Later he was
reduced to crawling as his only means of "going on," that is, continuing
physically and verbally; thus he labels himself a "crawling creator" as his
alternations of crawls and falls correspond to his periods of murmurings
and silences. Like the prose in the novel *How It Is,* where the character
along with his jagged language proceeds "piecemeal" in "midget grammar," details about his movements are worded carefully so that they can
be read as depictions of his verbal style as well:

> One two three four one. Knee hand knee hand two. Six. So on. In what
> he wills a beeline. Till having encountered no obstacle discouraged he
> heads back the way he came. From nought anew. Or in some quite
> different direction. In what he hopes a beeline. Till again with no dead
> end for his pains he renounces and embarks on yet another course.
> From nought anew. Well aware or little doubting how darkness may
> deflect. Withershins on account of the heart. Or conversely to shortest
> path convert deliberate veer. (Pp. 49–50)

The motion of "withershins," a zigzag wandering (retracing the "zigzag" steps in the preceding fiction, *Fizzles*), visually recalls Jung's labyrinthine paths of the subconscious, a psychological vocabulary Beckett was surely familiar with (which also may have shaped his metaphorical mazes in the metafictional story *Lost Ones*).

Here the repeated pun on the word "lying" for the hearer/speaker's static fictionalizing also superimposes physical and verbal journeys. As he contemplates attitudes of the body and latitudes of language he ponders "[w]hich in other words of all the innumerable ways of lying is likely to prove in the long run the most endearing" (p. 55), and he prides himself that "[f]rom time to time with unexpected grace you lie" (p. 61). Now that he lies fixed, one available activity consists of imagining what his possible positions or means of locomotion might be. Hence his journey, like Winnie's, becomes all mental, "gropings of the mind" (p. 23), and his main goal is—more directly in this recent dramatization than in earlier plays—to pin down the central Self.

Analogies between the Beckettian quester or wanderer on the one hand and primitive gurus and mystics on the other can be facile or dangerous, but they are just as compelling and provocative as they are risky. Both sets of searchers attempt to situate a stable point in a turning world through a special use of language, all the while realizing that it is not merely a specific physical place they seek. Joseph Campbell quotes a Sioux medicine man named Black Elk who experiences similar needs and discovers similar solutions to those of the figure in *Company,* and to Hamm and Winnie: "He had once in vision beheld himself standing 'on the highest mountain,' at 'the center of the world,' [then] added: 'But anywhere is the center of the world.' " This search for the core of one's being, for what the Hindus call the "indwelling Self," can be transformed into a rigorous and controlled psychological path to transcendence primarily through a type of Indian yoga,[30] and Beckett might indeed project this tradition onto the background of his drama since he included a yoga pose for balance, the tree, as one of the gestures for waiting in *Godot.* The Beckett hero is continuously and consciously trying to remain upright rather than falling into some ditch and to balance multiple binary forces: past and present, teller and told, inner and outer, mind and body.

Obsessed with his body, the figure in *Company* fixes its position with sensory impressions (which remain the only certainties) because he needs to feel the floor under his back in order to "verify" his existence. Thus he agonizes over whether to sit or to lie, to lie prone or supine, almost as if there were something magical about his orientation. As he tries to garner empirical evidence for functioning of mind as well as for presence of body, we realize that he must exercise far more skepticism than a Descartes: he cannot even say with certitude "I hear, therefore I am" since the surrounding voices are ambiguous, and there may be a second or third intended hearer. As a probable and active "Hearer," he calls up incidents from his past, far and near, but keeps reverting to his present metaphysical predicament; in other words, he mentally and stylistically circles around a midpoint usually regained after his forays into speculation and into recollection: the initial proposition that he is on his back in the dark—alone.

Also alone and surrounded by darkness, Krapp attended by his tapes has at least his magic spot in the circle of light above his desk, which he uses as a home base during *his* gropings of the mind, his wanderings through time aided by recorded words on tape: "The new light above my table is a great improvement. With all this darkness round me I feel less alone. *(Pause.)* In a way. *(Pause.)* I love to get up and move about in it, then back here to . . . *(hesitates)* . . . me. *(Pause.)* Krapp" (p. 15). Able to recenter himself literally and metaphorically, and thus more secure in his metaphysics than the protagonist in the monologue *Company,* Krapp senses that he is a series of selves fractured over time (*we* know how consistent those different ages and selves are) and that all he has to do is to tape and replay the past, mechanically to remember in words in order to "Be again" (p. 26). Less sure of anything, especially of being, the figure in *Company* is granted no proper name—only the generic "Figure" and "Hearer," an entity subject to Space and to Time respectively. Like the Unnamable (whose label he temporarily adopts), he seeks to attain that indisputable self, which Krapp—who is steps ahead of him in achievement of personal identity—could take for granted. *Company*'s figure yearns to hear "Yes, I remember," echoing Krapp's "Be again" ("I" corresponding to being, and "remember" to "again"). Only then could he feel at peace, having found—underneath and through and by all the words—his true identity for company.

It is perhaps significant that *Company*'s title indicates not a named character, or an unnamable creature, or a not I, but a state of being. This monologue, resembling that in *The Unnamable,* parallels one of the concepts of the *Bhagavad Gita,* that the Self is "[e]ternal, all-pervading, unchanging, immovable." The Hearer calls up several earlier personas, relationships, and actions—good, bad, and neutral—in hopes of focusing all his memories into an integrated, autonomous person who acted, who can say "Yes, I did; therefore I am." But no transcendence above mundane details ever occurs. An elevated and enduring union of man and the cosmos, argues Campbell,

is effected through a realization of the true relationship of the passing phenomena of time to the imperishable life that lives and dies in all. . . .
Man in the world of action loses his centering in the principle of eternity if he is anxious for the outcome of his deeds, but resting them

and their fruits on the knees of the Living God he is released by them, as by a sacrifice, from the bondages of the sea of death.[31]

Never attaining that ritualistic indwelling Self, Figure at least keeps trying, keeps using prose as helpers (words become almost palpable, much as the name "Godot" was a lifesaver the tramps could hold onto), continually evaluating which phrases might be the most "companionable."

Naturally enough, to express unsayable feelings on stage, Beckett was writing concurrently a drama that depends on no words at all, *Quad*. This mime (videotaped in 1981 and 1982) consists of four characters walking rapidly to drumbeats on the borders of four quadrants along various paths and patterns. We are transported all the way back before language and before drama—to gesture, dance, and music associated with re-enactments of a hunt; or to the unrecapturable first time when, in a Greek ritual tragedy (probably a ceremony for Dionysus), a chorus's measured steps would determine the metered "feet" of poetry. Beckett, in the notes for *Quad*, requests of the performers, "Some ballet training desirable"; here staccato movements supplant lyrical words.

Each player (wearing a different-colored hooded robe and followed by a matching-colored light) walks rapidly in varied configurations toward the center of the quad and away again repeatedly. Beckett doubled this form: actually there is a *Quad I* and a *Quad II*, with the replay dividing the pace of drum and footsteps in half. Repetition of the whole—like the reprise of *Play* verbatim—indicates the compulsion to continue a search, even if energy is running down. In both parts I and II, every time a player is almost at the midpoint (termed a "danger zone") he diverges from it by a quick turn to the left. Does this depict a fearful avoidance of the center or a frustrating inability to possess it? Either way, *Quad* is at one level portraying an aborted journey to an indwelling self. When Jung's schizophrenic patients were in therapy (creatures as split as Beckett's character in *Not I*, insisting that the autobiographical woman in her story is "she"), they invariably drew mandala pictures, sometimes including four quadrants but always based on concentric circles (a circumscribed personality?) lacking a center.[32] These revealing structures, uncannily similar in similar patients, contained designs that either negated a central area or never quite focused on the midpoint: ornaments and curlicues would veer away.[33] As their psychological conditions improved and their sense of self began to congeal, the quad drawings demonstrated increasingly more control toward an ordered nucleus. Beckett's characters, however, neither literally nor metaphorically, neither in word nor in gesture, neither for themselves nor for their artistic creations, can achieve the centering that brings order and peace.

By restricting the formal activity in *Quad* to a small performance area,

Beckett visually calls up the notion of an altar or ritual circle; and by choosing *four* figures, he can suggest the classical four points of the compass, four seasons, four epistles, four apocalyptic creatures, and such. Most significantly, by having the figures accumulate from 1 to 2 to 3 to 4 in disciplined, choreographed routines, Beckett sets up expectations for a ritualistic dance. But soon after all four players are present, they begin—incrementally—to disperse, no communal dance having occurred. This symmetrical and studied movement in accord with heavy percussion produces neither a somber tribal ceremony nor a joyous celebration, but rather an enforced sentence, a regulated torment, an imprisonment. "And, since the figures always turn left, not only at the centre but at all the corners also, the pattern is that of the damned in the Inferno."[34] In another country, in another century, four figures gathering around a center might have been preparing a redemptive sacrifice or welcoming the spring, dancing around a Maypole, for instance, as their symbolic focus of attention, performing a "forest ring," or dancing to celebrate or promote fertility.[35] In a precursor to *Quad* drafted in the 1960s and called *J. M. Mime,* Beckett's initial conception, Gontarski tells us, was to have two pairs of characters walking along quadrants in all the possible paths *starting* from 0 (a central origin) and *returning* to 0. But in its final realization almost twenty years later, the mime begins and ends with the void, an empty quad, and travelers deflect their steps *away* from "0." By the 1980s no centers are holding.

*   *   *

Beckett's dramatic characters have never been whole, centered people (for instance, Gogo/Didi and Hamm/Clov need each other as opposites to be complete), and in *That Time* and *Not I* stage space is severely skewed and decentered. Finally with *Quad* Beckett writes a work dramatizing, by the most palpable means, futile motion—psychological and metaphysical—around yet away from a center. In a universe of uncertainty but of cerain mortality, a world like Beckett's stage and near our own, we cannot take for granted the conventional values of goals, religions, quests. There are no Virgils, Merlins, or Obi Wan Kenobis—no helpers (and often no human companions at all) so that language itself must act as agent and fellow traveler. For the modern audience, attention shifts from endpoint to voyaging, from achievement to process, from climax to dialogue. Considering their scary predicaments and scarce resources, we can assess the persevering storytelling of Hamm and Hearer as heroic, and can realize that, although Mouth's attempts to begin a story fail repeatedly, "that struggle testifies to her heroism."[36] And James Knowlson argues that at its best Winnie's compulsive language "invests her with a muted form of brave heroism."[37] Beckett's use of the wanderer myth in his theater is similar, then, to Joyce's ironic overlay of Homer in *Ulysses:* at first the comparison makes the modern traveler, Leopold Bloom, appear diminished and ridiculous, but at some level the Homeric parallel may be taken seriously. In his own simple way Bloom *is* clever, wise, generous, admirable, hospitable, and, yes, even great. Chivalrous deeds are no longer possible for contemporary heroes, and indeed mere movement alone becomes exponentially rare on Beckett's stage: the most heroic task one can perform is to spend the arduous journey finding words, and the fact that Beckett's verbal wanderers speak so beautifully and valiantly—even in the face of infinite void—gives them mythic status through their poetic travel.

Notes

1. Sighle Kennedy, "Spirals of Need: Irish Prototypes in Samuel Beckett's Fiction," in *Yeats, Joyce, Beckett: New Light on Three Modern Irish Writers,* ed. Kathleen McGrory and John Unterecker (Lewisberg, Pa.: Bucknell University Press, 1976), p. 156.

2. See Deirdre Bair, *Samuel Beckett: A Biography* (New York: Harcourt Brace Jovanovich, 1978), pp. 177–78. The relationships between ritual and myth are many and complex, and cannot be disentangled here; but for a clear and succinct discussion—citing several central texts—see Stanley Edgar Hyman, "The Ritual View of Myth and the Mythic" in *Myth and Literature: Contemporary Theory and Practice,* ed. John B. Vickery (Lincoln: University of Nebraska Press, 1966). To compound the complexity, there is the hazy connection between ritual and the beginning of drama; one of the best discussions of this can be found in the introductory chapter of *Ur-Drama: The Origins of Theatre* by E. T. Kirby (New York: New York University Press, 1975).

3. Victor Turner, *Dramas, Fields, and Metaphors: Symbolic Action in Human Society* (Ithaca: Cornell University Press, 1974), p. 196.

4. Turner, p. 198.

5. A. J. Leventhal, "The Beckett Hero," in *Samuel Beckett: A Collection of Critical Essays,* ed. Martin Esslin (Englewood Cliffs, N.J.: Prentice-Hall, Inc., 1965), p. 43.

6. Samuel Beckett, *Waiting for Godot.* For the longer plays I refer to the individual Grove Press volumes. Page citations for *All That Fall, Cascando,* and *Footfalls* are from *Collected Shorter Plays* (New York: Grove Press, 1984).

7. Edith Kern, "Moran—Molloy: The Hero as Author," *Perspective,* 11, no. 3 (Autumn, 1959): 187–88.

8. Rubin Rabinovitz, "*Molloy* and the Archetypal Traveller," *Journal of Beckett Studies,* no. 5 (Autumn 1979): 31, 41.

9. Jean Yamasaki Toyama, "Malone, the Unoriginal Centre," *Journal of Beckett Studies,* no. 9 (1984): 89–99.

10. Ludovic Janvier, "Place of Narration/Narration of Place," in *Samuel Beckett: A Collection of Criticism,* ed. Ruby Cohn (New York: McGraw-Hill, 1975), p. 104.

11. Janvier, p. 105.

12. Rabinovitz, p. 33.

13. John J. Sheedy, "The Comic Apocalypse of King Hamm," *Modern Dramas,* 9 (Dec. 1966): 316–17.

14. Turner, pp. 182, 193.

15. Joseph Campbell, *The Hero With a Thousand Faces* (Princton: Princeton University Press, 1949), pp. 91–92.

16. Thomas R. Simone, "'Faint, though by no means invisible,' A Commentary on Beckett's *Footfalls*," *Modern Drama*, 26 (Dec. 1983): 435–46.

17. Pierre Chabert, "The Body in Beckett's Theatre," *Journal of Beckett Studies*, no. 8 (Autumn 1982): 26, 27.

18. Hersh Zeifman, "Religious Imagery in the Plays of Samuel Beckett," *Samuel Beckett; A Collection of Criticism*, ed. Ruby Cohn (New York: McGraw-Hill, 1975), p. 90.

19. David J. Alpaugh, "The Symbolic Structure of Samuel Beckett's *All That Fall*," *Modern Drama*, 9 (Dec. 1966): 329.

20. Sidney Homan, *Beckett's Theatres: Interpretations for Performance* (London and Toronto: Associated University Presses, 1984), pp. 122–27.

21. Sheedy, pp. 311–312.

22. Campbell, *The Hero*, p. 261.

23. Christopher Innes, *Holy Theatre: Ritual and the Avant Garde* (Cambridge: Cambridge University Press, 1981), pp. 213–14.

24. Paul Lawley, "Symbolic Structure and Creative Obligation in *Endgame*," *Journal of Beckett Studies*, no. 5 (Autumn 1979): 52–53.

25. Lawley, p. 57.

26. This information and other ideas on Asian drama and Eastern ritual come from Prof. Carol Fisher Sorgenfrei, Theatre Arts Department, UCLA, in personal communication.

27. Homan, p. 81.

28. Ruby Cohn, *Just Play: Beckett's Theater* (Princeton: Princeton University Press, 1981), p. 27.

29. Victor Turner, *From Ritual to Theatre: The Human Seriousness of Play* (New York: Performing Arts Journal Publications, 1982), pp. 52–58.

30. Joseph Campbell, *The Mythic Image* (Princeton: Princeton University Press, 1974), pp. 280, 278.

31. Campbell, *The Hero*, pp. 238–39.

32. I did not know about this work of Jung's when I intuited for an earlier paper on ritual that *Quad* characters trace mandalas on the stage floor. See "'My Shade Will Comfort You': Beckett's Rites of Theater," in *Samuel Beckett*, ed. Patrick McCarthy (Boston: G. K. Hall, 1986).

33. See illustrations in Campbell, *Mythic Image*, pp. 338, 365.

34. S. E. Gontarski, "'Quad I & II'; Beckett's Sinister Mime(s)" (review of play production), *Journal of Beckett Studies*, no. 9 (1984): 137.

35. Gerardus Van de Leeuw, *Sacred and Profane Beauty: The Holy in Art*, trans. David E. Green (New York: Holt, Rinehart, 1963), p. 13.

36. Elin Diamond, "The fictionalizers in Beckett's Plays," in *Samuel Beckett: A Collection of Criticism*, ed. Ruby Cohn (New York: McGraw-Hill, 1975), pp. 116, 119.

37. James Knowlson and John Pilling, *Frescoes of the Skull: The Later Prose and Drama of Samuel Beckett* (New York: Grove Press, 1980), p. 102.

From the Perspective
of an Actress/Critic

Ritual Patterns in Beckett's Happy Days

Martha Fehsenfeld

As everyone knows, all of Samuel Beckett's characters are in a trap of one kind or another. In *Happy Days,* Winnie's is a mound of scorched earth. She is the remains of a life buried in a premature grave. Beckett told me, "Think of her as a bird with oil on her feathers." A bird unable to fly, a creature of the air kept by some irrevocable, determined force out of her natural element, unlike Willie who is trapped in his. She yearns to fly, speaks of nightingales, of floating up into the blue. Her arms are wings but they are useless; they have let her down—they won't take her up. She stares into the azure but she can't join it. She sings her song like the thrush or the bird of dawning, but she can't soar as they can. She is trapped in the ground. Grounded. She can only reach for the sky and remember when she was free as air.

So grounded, Winnie can only go through the motions of living out her days, and these inevitably become ritualized vestiges of what was—of all that is left. Ritual in Beckett is always closely related to pain. It is an alternative to pain—the only choice available in an otherwise closed system of determined suffering. Often as in *Waiting for Godot* or *Endgame,* it takes the form of games. In *Happy Days,* it seems to be Winnie's attempt to divert her mind from the external circumstances which confront her: to engage the mind in a game which distracts her from the awareness of her suffering, from the condition of her body—its deterioration. The pain is constant, so in order to accomplish this diversion, she has to interrupt its pattern, however briefly, by creating another pattern. But because this pain is continuous, it breaks through during those moments when energy or opportunity or circumstance must of necessity stop the game momentarily. Winnie's greatest fear is that when she runs out of words or out of games, the consciousness of her suffering will resume and the pattern of the pain predominate.

The game that chiefly occupies Winnie in the first act is the one she plays with the objects in her bag. I became aware of the importance of those "things" as I began to work on the part in 1983, and I discovered that except for the vital presence of Willie, there was no one else with whom to play. These objects became, in a sense, my co-players. I spoke to them, I addressed them, and in their presence they responded in a strange way. They were my only props even as they were Winnie's, and as I wrote to Beckett, they became my friends. Even as one lying in bed or otherwise immobilized fingers the object nearest to him in a very personal way, so does Winnie, seeing them up close from the limited perspective of her world. They become inhabitants of that world she seeks to know intimately. I came to know first hand what Beckett meant when he had Winnie say, ". . . *things* have a life."[1]

Winnie also plays games with time. Beckett wrote in his rehearsal notebook for the 1979 production with Billie Whitelaw, "Relate frequency of broken speech and action to discontinuity of time. Time experience incomprehensible transport from one inextricable present to the next. Those past unremembered those to come inconceivable."[2] And he referred in the 1979 rehearsals of the play to ". . . this time business she has on the brain. . . ."[3]

Time is not only on her brain; it is in the title of the play and is threaded throughout its text. The emblem of time—the bell, "like a knife on metal,"[4] begins and ends the play. "She has three seconds to obey the bell. If she hasn't obeyed, it goes again."[5] Winnie's first line is "Another heavenly day," followed by her habitual devotions and bow to the Deity. Her toothpaste is "running out": it's "one of those old things." She calls upon her memory again and again to bring back things forgotten, half-remembered, half-forgotten. She is caught not only in the earth, but in the inevitable unyielding *now* of the present. Everything that is possible is in the past: "those wonderful lines," "the fleeing joys," "the happy memories," "the happy days."

Willie is there, from time to time, in the *now*, but he is not with her; they are separated in space by disparate elements. All of the good memories—the happy days with him—are in the past, retrievable only through memory. And as long as they stay in the past, "when [she] had the use of [her] legs," she is protected, but when the conscious awareness of the now breaks through this insulation, she is exposed and vulnerable to the pain she feels and can no longer deny. Beckett indicates this in the 1979 rehearsal notebook, commenting on the breakdowns that Winnie suffers—"the defaillances"—and the stillness that always follows, "And now?" Beckett also stressed the celebratory aspect of "that day" Winnie refers to in "Golden you called it, that day, the last guest gone . . ." (p. 24), saying to Billie: "Here you take a strand of hair between the thumb and forefinger of your left hand, pick up an imaginary glass with your right hand. Scoop up to toast in silence . . . try to get the feeling he's drinking a toast to her hair . . . that holy day."[6]

The first act establishes a quality of interruption. Beckett, whose direction is always concerned with the rhythm of the ritual, maintained that this was "a clue of the play—something begins, something else begins. Winnie is constantly being interrupted or is interrupting herself. She is an interrupted being."[7] These interruptions by Winnie and Willie were directed in counterpoint during the business of Willie's turning the pages of his newspaper in harmony with Winnie's business with her hat; and later when Beckett instructed Billie to put down her glass and toothbrush as Willie put down his newspaper, he said, "Try to get the music in that. They all go slowly down together."[8] It was essential for Winnie on a purely practical level that Willie do exactly the same thing exactly the same way each time, as Willie was always seated away from Winnie and couldn't depend upon sight cues.

Repetition was, of course, a key element in both rehearsal and performance and recalled Beckett's often-quoted observation to Charles Marowitz: "Producers don't seem to have any sense of form in movement, the kind of form one finds in music, for instance, where themes keep recurring. When, in a text, actions are repeated, they ought to be made unusual the first time, so that when they happen again—in exactly the same way—an audience will recognize them from before."[9] Beckett emphasized Winnie's reaction to Willie's rejection: "Once you've established the way of saying it, you say it the same way each time as in 'NO? You don't?' and 'No? You won't?' It's as if you were prepared for his negative response."[10] And then he assured Billie that, when Winnie says "The old style. . . ," "remember that you say it so often the movement says it for you. It could almost be inaudible." When as Winnie I arrived at those moments in the text when phrases are repeated, I decided on a particular movement, gesture, or attitude, together with a specific vocal quality, to achieve as close a duplication as possible from one moment to another. I found the tape recorder extremely helpful, too, as had Billie Whitelaw in 1979. And I became aware of the repetitive aspect of the rehearsal process itself— another practical ritual always available to any Beckett actor, as it is indigenous to every Beckett play: the doing of it over and over again was there to be exploited and I exploited it. Over and over, during my rehearsals and performances.

The rhythm of the ritual, whether it involves the precision of gesture or word is central to Beckett's approach to the play. One can see the importance of this rhythm as Beckett sets forth the relationship between Winnie and her bag and the consequent specified activity in his 1979 rehearsals with Billie Whitelaw.

The bag is all she has—look at it with affection. . . From the first you should know how she feels about it . . . When the bag is at the right height you peer in, see what things are there and then get them out. Peer, take, place. Peer, take, place. You peer more when you pick things up than when you put them down. Everything has its place.[11]

The meticulous designation of the right and left hand and the location in the use of each prop was scrupulously patterned in the notebook and further extended in rehearsal. Both Beckett and Billie worked to achieve the ease and precision of the motions. They worked out a swooping gesture in which hands would extend clawlike up and then down into the recesses of the bag, retrieving the object and putting it to use.[12] First rehearsals were marked by deepest concentration and near silence as Billie sat at her table-mound onstage, Beckett seated directly opposite, he whispering the lines from memory, she watching his mouth form the words, repeating them, copying him as if she were looking at herself in a mirror. As I sat in the back row of the theatre watching them, I felt as if I were eavesdropping on a secret ceremony of some kind, observing a ritual of a ritual.

When I worked on the role four years later, I soon realized that the ritual involved not only the rhythm of movement, but the rhythmic relationship of word and movement. The Olympian challenge of separating word and movement, one of my problems as I worked on the role, gradually became assimilated into the character as I learned to go *with* the offbeat, syncopated rhythms instead of *against* them. I subsequently realized to my joy that, rather than the frantic frenetic movement which I had feared would result, there were actually rests built into the score of the text. My body began to learn to sing the music of *Happy Days* along with my voice.

While playing Winnie, I had to discover the center of my own energy. In act 1, it was at the base of my spine—the pivotal point between right and left, using my arms for balance while I moved from the waist from side to side as the corrected text directed. (Beckett based his single, double, and triple turns on this fulcrum principle, which he specified in the annotated text he prepared for The National Theatre production in London in 1974 for Dame Peggy Ashcroft.) In act 2, it was at the base of my skull that I found the point of greatest tension and my inward "turning point." Having discovered this, I was then able to attain a measure of relaxation, not unlike the "rests" mentioned above that Beckett seemed to have built into the text. And with the centering I could consequently designate certain points along an imaginary, semicircular curve from one eye to the other.

Unlike act 1, in which there are exit routes planned, albeit false ones, in act 2 the only escape mechanism Winnie has is her story. Mildred's story that begins in the womb. As I plotted its action, I chose a spot within my righthand field of vision where the mouse was. As long as I could avert my eyes from that spot, Winnie and I were safe. But in the telling of the story, Winnie's confrontation with both the word and the spot were inevitable. I had to say the word and look at its image. Winnie tries to divert herself from pain by retrieving the once-forgotten story, but in this remembering she also remembers the pain it contains, and ritual becomes her snare instead of her only way out.

I was also able to use this centering of the face during the recital of the Shower-Cooker story a little later on in the same act—the narrowed-down echo of the story in act 1 on the same subject. I isolated first one side and then the other, using my cheek, lips, and mouth muscles, speaking first with the man's voice and then with the woman's. I decided on the central part of my face as the focus of Winnie's neutral voice in the narrative. Described later by a member of the audience, the result was as if a rubberlike mask had been pulled first to one side and then to the other. I attempted to use the right and left parts of my face in a way analogous to my right and left upper body and arms in the preceding act.

The eyes were, of course, of enormous importance in this act. The side gazes required a use of the eye muscles in an intense, highly concentrated manner. Everything was narrowed in, contained, right. All my responses were limited to the strongest possible kinds of reaction, which were then registered on my face. The ritual was closely observed, often unbearably so. I have never felt my body so confined and my mind so active simultaneously.

But even as precision of movement and voice are a key to the ritual of *Happy Days,* another essential quality of the ritual is the element of mystery. One recalls Beckett's well-known statement in a letter to Jessica Tandy in 1971 when he referred to *Not I:* "I am not unduly concerned with intelligibility. I hope the piece may work on the nerves of the audience not its intellect."[13] In *Happy Days* we are moved into this area of mystery, beginning in the first act, and we experience its deepening in the second, when, as Beckett says, ". . . the dark moves in."[14] We don't know why Winnie is where she is, or how long she'll stay there, or why we see her from the waist up in act 1 and from the neck up in act 2, but we accept it because this is the image before us. Beckett confronts us by stating this inexplicable image as fact. "Strangeness," Beckett informs us, "was the necessary condition of the play—of Winnie's plight in the play."[15] During Berlin rehearsals Beckett said, "In this play you have the combination of the strange and the practical, the mysterious and the factual. This is the crux of both the comedy and the tragedy in it."[16] The play ends in deliberate, mysterious circumstances of intentional ambiguity. We don't know if Willie is going for the gun or for Winnie's face. We accept the image of the outstretched hand midway between. We accept the mystery before us.

Finally, I have come to realize that merely saying Beckett takes you from safe places to unsafe places is very different from experiencing such a journey as an actress. There is a great deal about endurance in the play and about real fear. The way to the truth of this "real fear" can be found in the mechanics and the ritual of the performance itself. You are by yourself out there. Willie is onstage, but the actor playing the part can no more come to the aid of the actress playing Winnie than can the character himself. You are alone for that hour and a half. You are on the high wire and there is no safety net. But there is one device that keeps you from falling: the balance pole, that is, the text—the words and the music which are Winnie's only support, and the ritual of singing them as performed by Winnie and by the actress who plays her.

Notes

1. Samuel Beckett, *Happy Days* (New York: Grove Press, 1961), p. 54. All further references are to this edition.

2. Manuscript production notebook for Beckett's own production of *Glückliche Tage (Happy Days)* at the Schiller-Theater, Werkstatt, Berlin, 1971. RUL MS 1396/4/10, p. 62.

3. Martha Fehsenfeld, Rehearsal Diary of the 1979 Royal Court Theatre, London production.

4. Ibid.

5. Ibid.

6. Ibid.

7. Ibid.

8. Ibid.

9. Ruby Cohn, *Back to Beckett* (Princeton: Princeton University Press, 1973), p. 188.

10. Ibid.

11. Fehsenfeld.

12. Beckett showed consistant concern with the position of Winnie's hands throughout rehearsals. In his notebook he specified her opening position prior to her prayer, "Head back, hands clasp, eyes closed. S. M. [single movement] Lips 3". Text, eye o. [open] Head back level, hands toward mound, s.m. freeze before completion and after prayer." He circled "Head back, hands clasp" and put an arrow to a further statement, "in view of A8." A8 denotes the end of act 1 when Winnie tries unsuccessfully to pray. Production notebooks of Sammuel Beckett, *Happy Days: Sammuel Beckett's Production Notebook,* ed. James Knowlson (London: Faber and Faber, 1985), p. 36.

13. Verified in conversation with author, May 1978, New York. Note error in Deirdre Bair, *Samuel Beckett: A Biography* (New York: Harcourt Brace Jovanovich, 1978), p. 625.

14. Fehsenfeld.

15. Ibid.

16. Alfred Hübner, *Samuel Beckett inszeniert Glückliche Tage, Probenprotokoll Von Alfred Hubner* (Frankfurt: Suhrkamp Verlag, 1976).

To Speak the Words of "The Tribe"

The Wordlessness of Samuel Beckett's Metaphysical Clowns

Rosette C. Lamont

"No words for what when words gone"[1]

Among the numerous approaches to the problem of mythical thinking, that of Ernst Cassirer, in his *Philosophy of Symbolic Forms,* has been called "the most significant attempt of modern times to construct a philosophy of myth as an integral part of a philosophy of culture."[2] Cassirer emphasizes the nonrational aspect of the mythopoeic mind as it seeks to evolve a self-contained form of the interpretation of reality. In his short preliminary study, *Sprache und Mythos* [Language and Myth], Cassirer endeavors to come to grips with the problem of the archaic mode of thought underlying both language and the grammar of art forms. Although he privileged language as the means of breaking the bounds of the myth-making phase of human mentality, he believed that language and myth should be seen as aspects of "the same miracle of the spirit. . . ."[3] In his evolving theory of mental activity Cassirer placed linguistic and mythical thinking within the same category, one viewed as being at variance with logical thought and discursive process. In the prelogical mode thought does not range over the data of intuition; it "is captivated and enthralled by the intuition which suddenly confronts it."[4] However, this intuition must be given symbolic expression in order to be fixed in consciousness. Cassirer concludes that "myth and language play similar roles in the evolution of thought from momentary experience to enduring conceptions, from sense impression to formulation, and that their respective functions are mutually conditioned.[5]

Although Cassirer's transition from the "Metaphysical principle of cosmic sympathy to the notion of the solidarity of human society"[6] is too optimistic a view for the second half of the twentieth century, his analysis

56

of the crisis in the development of language closely parallels Samuel Beckett's apprehension, particularly as it expresses itself in the wordless sketches for stage and television, and in his silent work for the screen, *Film*. In these short pieces Beckett returns to a condition which preceded the notion of language as a symbolic form. He sets language aside in order to achieve an archaic simplicity, a universality which allows the audience to travel in the direction of the unconscious, the prelogical, prelinguistic expression of "the tribe."

Beckett's silent clowns are like primitive men who explore the world at every turn. The mysterious preternatural forces are much in evidence, imparting a sense of danger, a feeling of amazement, but what is absent is the tragic sense that "the real protagonist is the order of God. . . ."[7] There is, of course, the mythic apprehension that "only death can end the tragic ambivalence of human nature,"[8] but the vaudeville form it receives in *Act Without Words I* and *Act Without Words II* lends it an ironic coloring. Although the scissors, palm tree, tiny carafe of water, and cubes that descend from the flies and then disappear *(Act Without Words I),* and the pointed goad issuing from the wings to prod awake A and B, asleep in their sacks *(Act Without Words II),* may appear as mysterious, uncanny, or even full of *mana* to the protagonists, we, the audience, perceive that they are obviously mechanistic. Thus, there is no reality set on fire by man's imagination, but a series of absurd defeats. The clown may experience what happens to him much as the primitive reacts to magic, but we, the viewer of his plan, seeking its simplistic origins, laugh even as we pity him.

If, in the world of myth, "man must be more than the victim of forces outside him, he must be their imaginative master,"[9] then Beckett's universe is composed of failed rituals. Yet the sense of ritual pervades these silent, mimetic enactments, as though on the edge of the abyss, in the face of want, death, and destruction, one still had to erect a simulacrum of safety through repetition. *Act Without Words I,* despite the unsuccessful suicide attempt near the end, dramatizes the human effort to survive in a hostile environment and the desire to understand that environment. *Act Without Words II* shows that life must be endured, if not understood. There are no triumphs, no resolution since the mercy of God, or his judgment, are absent. There is no control over the process, no understanding of it. The *hybris* of the insignificant creatures presented on the stage is not purged by their suffering; yet, by witnessing their suffering, so much like our own in its absurdity, we do undergo a classical catharsis, a catharsis through laughter and terror, pity and hopelessness.

If the two *Acts Without Words* focus on the process of living, *Film* deals with the apprenticeship to death, the process of detaching oneself from life. Like the Tibetan *Book of the Dead,* it teaches the gradual dissolution of self. The veiling of the windows and mirrors, the covering of the bird cage—the extinction of light, reflection, and life—are so many ritualistic steps to be taken before the final immobility, the resignation of the end. It is no accident that Beckett chose Buster Keaton as the protagonist of his "silent" film since Keaton established his reputation in the early days of cinema, before sound. Nor is it surprising that a basically comic actor should have created, at the end of his own life, a great tragic role, since for Beckett tragedy and comedy interfuse and overlap. *Film* is one of Beckett's most clearly ritualistic works, a slowly paced entrance into Thanatos.

"Esse est percipi,"[10] to be is to be perceived; Bishop Berkeley's maxim, inscribed at the top of Beckett's scenario for *Film,* could serve as the epigraph to all of his novels, novellas, plays, and pantomines. The first act of *Waiting for Godot* has Vladimir handing the following injunction to the Boy who seems to have appeared out of nowhere: "Tell him . . . *(he hesitates)* . . . tell him you saw us. *(Pause.)* You did see us, didn't you?"[11] To be seen or not to be seen, that is the question. But who is doing the perceiving? Beckett's characters are often left to wonder whether there is anyone other than their inner, thinking self, their double? The Narrator of *The Unnamable* raises such a possibility: "They depart, one by one, and the voices go on, it's not theirs, they were never there, there was never anyone but you, talking to you about you. . . ."[12] Is the writer then a supreme ventriloquist, or perhaps merely a transparent consciousness allowing for the voices of all the others to filter through? To speak the words of "the tribe," to become spoken rather than be speaking, such is the trap that language sets for the writer. Perhaps it is in an effort "to lend a purer meaning to the words of the tribe"[13] that Beckett tends towards silence, wordlessness.

For a writer whose whole existence is one of linguistic ubiquity, the interweaving and overlapping of English and French, and of the many literatures which constitute the richness of Beckettian thought, the striving for an existential poetry, one that would signify by means of universal gestures, is an extreme kind of denudation. The seeds of this project are present already in the "Three Dialogues" with Georges Duthuit, three conversations about the painters Tal Coat, Masson, and Bram Van Velde. Speaking of the latter, Beckett says that Van Velde was "the first to admit that to be an artist is to fail, as no other dare fail. . . ."[14] We recognize here an echo from Mallarmé, who also thought that a great artist must be a sublime *raté.* Limited goals and self satisfaction are the death of excellence; in this as in so many ways Beckett is Mallarmé's heir.

Whether written for the stage, the screen, or television, Beckett's plays without words concretize Mallarmé's dream of reproducing "en un milieu nul ou à peu près les grandes poses humaines et comme notre plastique morale" (". . . to reproduce in the space of nowhere, or thereabout, great human attitudes and our spiritual plasticity").[15] For the symbolist poet, ballet was "la forme théâtrale de poésie par excellence" (". . . poetry's theatrical form par excellence"),[16] and the ballet dancer a poem "dégagé de tout appareil du scribe" (". . . a poem free of the scribe's apparatus").[17] Pantomine, which Mallarmé also admired, had a good deal in common with dancing in that it was a form of prewriting, a statement that left the page unmarred, virginally white. When speaking of Paul Margueritte's "Pierrot Assassin de sa Femme," Mallarmé praises his "soliloque muet que, tout du long à son âme tient et du visage et des gestes le fantôme blanc comme une page pas encore écrite" (". . . a mute soliloquy delivered to his soul by the white phantom's face and gestures, like a yet unwritten page").[18] Allusive and elusive, pantomine creates "un milieu, pur, de fiction" ("a milieu of fiction, pure . . ."),[19] one that translates feelings and emotions by means of "phrases non proférées" ("unuttered pronouncements").[20] This wordless art has the immediacy and purity of music. Mallarmé makes this point in decribing the art of Legrand, an actor known for "shading the farcical with the dramatic":[21]

> Le silence, seul luxe après les rimes, un orchestre ne faisant avec son or, ses frôlements de soirs et de cadence, qu'en détailler la signification à l'égal d'une ode, tue et que c'est au poéte, suscité par le défi, de traduire! le silence que je cherche aux après-midi de musique, je l'ai trouvé avec contentement aussi, devant la réapparition toujours inédite comme lui-même, de Pierre, c'est à dir du clair et sagace mime Paul Legrand.

> (Silence, the only true luxury after poetry, an orchestra's gold, its twilight cadenced grazings detailing its significance, like a silent ode which the poet, rising to the challenge, must translate! the silence I seek at afternoon concerts, I found it also with deep satisfaction at the ever self-renewed, original reappearance of Pierre, that is to say the lucid and wise mime Paul Legrand.)[22]

Beckett's *Act Without Words I, Act Without Words II,* and *Film* seem to issue from this aesthetic.

Subtitled *A Mime for One Player, Act Without Words I* is a translation by the author of his *Acte sans paroles* and was performed by Deryk Mendel at the Royal Court Theatre of London on 3 April 1957. The play is a parable of resignation, a state one reaches only after a series of disappointments. The protagonist, one of Beckett's typical gentlemen tramps,[23] is an *expulsé* ("The Expulsed").[24] We see him thrust back from the right wing into an empty space, a desert bathed in "dazzling light."[25] There is no respite from this brilliance, and when, finally, he comes tumbling in, "flung backwards" (p. 125), it appears that this universe without shadows or shade is like a steady, pitiless gaze. Unlike the narrator of "The Expulsed," the unhappy creature of *Act I* does not bother raising his eyes to heaven whence assistance is supposed to issue. A number of objects, however, descend from "flies" (p. 126), each a puzzlement and a disappointment.

A meager world will slowly form itself about the prostrate man, then disappear, as though created and uncreated by an irrational power. The latter is represented by a sharp, inhuman, disembodied whistle coming either from the wings, or from above, depending on the direction of the propelling, moving force. Thus, the man's first explosion from the right wing, sending him tumbling out, is followed by the whistle. Recovering from the fall, the bewildered creature takes the sound for some kind of call, and, after a bit of reflection, proceeds in that direction only to find himself hurled back again. Next, the sound issues from the left. The scene is repeated in reverse. It becomes clear, as far as the man is concerned, and the audience as well, that the only space available will be the one we are shown; this is a "no exit" situation. In just a matter of a few seconds Beckett has concretized man's being in the world. The tumbling stumblings of this clown illustrate Kierkegaard's apprehension in regard to thought's inability to reach existence.

The protagonist of *Act I* is not a mindless creature. On the contrary, Beckett tells us over and over again in his stage directions that he thinks, reflects, and continues to reflect. One can detect here, as in so many other works of Beckett, a caricature of Descartes's *cogito*. As Hugh Kenner states: "Cartesian man deprived of his bicycle is a mere intelligence fastened to a dying animal."[26] Moreover, Beckett's clownish protagonist's reason is surrounded by a Jasperian and Heideggerian existence, a paltry but unavoidable *Umgreifende*.

First we witness the descent of a tree, seemingly falling from the sky, a caricature of the Tree of Life. Its single bough and tufted top cast a spidery shadow on the ground. The man would not have been cognizant of this presence were it not for the same sharp whistle calling his attention, as though an angel or a god blew a police whistle. Thus summoned, the lone protagonist looks from this unexpected object to "his hands" (p. 126), as though noticing his own body for the first time. Although his face remains expressionless one detects a measure of amazement at being there, *en situation,* at being. Having become cognizant of his *Dasein,* Beckett's clown-man will accept the presence of various *Seiendes,* as Heidegger calls existing objects. The next one, once again announced by the same imperious, monotonously shrill whistle, is a pair of scissors. The man, sitting comfortably in the lacy shade of his tree, proceeds to trim his nails. There is something pathetic and comical at once about this intimate act of personal grooming, one performed for no other reason than the sudden availability of the correct object. The scissors of course could stand for any other useful object of daily living, such as a house or car, objects whose "thereness" is most often taken for granted. But whereas in Heidegger there is no *Seiendes* without a *Sein,* the objects of *Act I* are not only independent of the man who perceives them, but perverse and unaccountably elusive. As the short sketch unfolds upon the stage we see a prereflective *cogito* in action, but this innocent will learn not to trust things. Not that the innocence of Beckett's clownish protagonist is that of primitive man; rather we are made to witness modern man in a world of articles of consumption. There is nothing particular about the scissors, for example; they are one of those products supplied *en masse,* the need for which might not have predated their appearance. Not so, however, in the case of the bottle bearing the large label WATER which will dangle before our thirsty hero, always out of reach.

The rest of the sketch is a study in frustrated efforts. Cubes descend, large and small. Like a trained monkey, the protagonist will attempt to place one on top of the other in order to reach the desired object. He will proceed by trial and error, first putting the large cube on top of the small one, and falling on the ground when attempting to scale this inverted pyramid, then creating the correct structure only to see the carafe yanked up beyond his grasp. Beckett seems to have a wonderful time deriding scientific inquiry, empirical investigations. Man the scientist is perhaps the butt of this ironic image.

As the carafe remains out of reach, a knotted rope descends, announced by the now familiar whistle. Our "hero" contemplates it for a while. The impression conveyed is that of a monkey held in a mad scientist's cage. But Beckett's *homo sapiens* is not lost in thought for a long time; he begins his ascent. At the moment he is about to reach his goal, in this case the delightful carafe of water, the rope is let out, and the climber comes down with a slam. Not only has Beckett succeeded in re-creating a circus performance, but he has concretized human ambition.

The scissors will now be put to quite a different use. The protagonist decides to cut a length of rope. As he begins to do so, the rope is yanked up together with its cutter, but not before our clown-hero succeeds in his endeavor to the extent of falling down together with his bit of rope. The scissors also come tumbling after. Beckett's protagonist then fashions a lasso in a final bold attempt to bring down the desired object, but at that moment the carafe "is pulled up quickly and disappears in flies" (p. 130).

With his last hope out of sight the protagonist's thoughts turn to making his quietus. Because no word is spoken, the man's determination takes the form of concerted effort. He looks at the bough of the single tree, "lasso in hand" (p. 130), brings over the cubes, goes through the charade of setting them on top of one another, first seemingly ready to make his past mistake, then, having acquired bitter experience, placing the smaller cube atop the large one. He is about to swing the lasso onto the bough when the tree folds like a parasol. This particular suicide plan is foiled. The scene echos the discussion Gogo and Didi have under their solitary tree:

ESTRAGON: Let's hang ourselves immediately!
VLADIMIR: From a bough? (*They go towards the tree.*)
                   I wouldn't trust it.

ESTRAGON: We can always try.
VLADIMIR: Go ahead.
ESTRAGON: After you.

(P. 12)

They decide it is safer to do nothing. The protagonist of *Act I* does not wish to play safe; he has no choice.

As he goes back and forth, setting the cubes in their places, he is still thinking. His fingering of the scissors, testing them for sharpness, loosening of his shirt collar, and the way in which he touches his neck are the eloquent if mute discourses of a man determined to leave his life. Beckett's would-be suicides, however, are as ineffectual as Chekhov's antiheroes. Their guns may not misfire, but here, for example, the small cube on which the desperate man, having trimmed his nails for the last time, sets down the rope and scissors, is pulled up. Chances for death are as elusive as life's rare opportunities. As the disheartened protagonist collapses on the big cube, it is "pulled from under him" (p. 132). He falls on his side, facing the audience, undone.

The end of the pantomine is a picture of despair, a quiet desperation which manifests itself as complete indifference. The prostrate man does not react any longer to any stimuli. The imperative whistle can not goad him to action; neither the carafe which has reappeared and dangles close to his face, nor the tree unfolding again and casting its shadow over his body get a rise out of him. Soon, both carafe and tree are yanked up by the same invisible, capricious power. The man is left alone. "He looks at his hands" (p. 133). The last line suggests an imprisonment within the confines of one's body. All is gone, except this mortal flesh which has escaped mortality for a while longer.

But who percieved this struggling creature full of reason and hope, finally full of quiet despair? Some elusive ironist seemed to mock him. Only when he gave up wanting, trying, reaching, was the protagonist of *Act I* left alone, left to his solitude. He had to still within himself the voice of modest desires. There is perhaps a kind of Buddhist lesson in this short play, or perhaps an echo of the melancholy spirit of Schopenhauer, of a denial of the will-to-life. Beckett's triumph lies in having embodied his *Weltanschauung* in a touching, grotesque, Pierrot-like figure.

The same kind of character, accompanied by his opposite double, appears in *Act Without Words II*, "a mime for two players." It is the abstract image of one day in the life of two men of contrasting temperaments.

At first we are shown two sacks stage right, A and B, with a small pile of clothes (C) neatly folded (coat and trousers surmounted by boots and hat).[27] Beckett specifies that the mime is to be played upon a long and narrow platform at the back of the stage, with the rest of the stage space in darkness. What is created is a "frieze effect" (p. 137). Since the sacks are inhabited—one man to a sack—we witness once again a "no-exit" situation. The entire stage space might be viewed as the world space where the two men occupy a restricted, circumscribed zone. Their progress is linear, from one end of the narrow platform to the other (right to left); it represents one day in their existence, or perhaps the course of their entire life. Besides, for Beckett, movement to the left suggests the walk of Dante and Virgil in the *Inferno*.[28]

No one sees the men, nor do they ever set eyes on one another. There is, however, an impersonal force that brings each one out of his particular bag—a goad mounted on a single wheel. This goad is not unlike the shrill whistle of *Act I*. When A issues from his bag, B is asleep within his own "dwelling." The pile of clothing (C) is visibly shared by both men but they seem to be unaware of this fact. This lack of perception is puzzling since B stacks his clothes neatly while A leaves them scattered when he crawls back into his bag; neither registers surprise at seeing the state of his clothing upon awakening. Also, neither A nor B appears to realize that each one of them carries the other on his back when they move the two bags from the right wing to the left; they take their burden for granted.

Were A and B roommates they would form the "Odd Couple." A broods, takes pills, eats his carrot without appetite, "spits it out with disgust" (p. 138), broods again, and prays after crawling out of his sack and before crawling back in. He is a moper, a dreamer, perhaps a poet. B is a very different kind of man: grotesquely efficient, a workaholic, a health nut. He exercises, rubs his scalp, combs his hair, consults a watch, a map, a compass. He is, in fact, a kind of Pozzo, perhaps a businessman, an executive. If the hypochondriacal dreamer is ridiculous, so is the maniacally meticulous, narcissistic, fastidious *homme moyen,* hardly *sensuel.* Both end up in their bags.

No words are necessary to convey the futility of man's passage on this earth. Beckett's vision could be said to belong to the early stages of the development of myth and ritual, when man could hope at best for "an uneasy truce between himself and chaos, because the cycle merely returned to its beginnings."[29] Beckett says it all by means of his mime plays. His gestural vocabulary corresponds perfectly to what Baudelaire defines in *De l'essence du rire* as "l'élemént comique pur, dégagé et concentré" ("the pure comic element, free and concentrated").[30]

Beckett's wordless plays are the perfect vehicle for their author's ironic sense of humor. The question most often asked is, "Are they really funny? Does one laugh? What kind of laughter is elicited?" There is no simple answer since Beckett's laugh, or that of his many clown-heroes, is a grimace, somewhere between soundless merriment and mute sobbing. In

Malone meurt, the narrator declares: "Je suis né grave comme d'autres syphilitiques" ("I was born grave as others syphilitic").[31] Seriousness, however, hardly precludes the ability to joke, particularly at one's own expense. The laughter favored by Beckett is a joyless expression coming from the groin, what he calls the "*risus purus,* the laugh laughing at the laugh, the beholding, the saluting of the highest joke, in a word the laugh that laughs—silence please—at that which is unhappy."[32] Clearly, only the grotesque, according to this definition, can hope to attain to what Baudelaire, whom Beckett echoes, calls "le comique absolu" in *De l'essence du rire.*[33] The laughter Baudelaire envisioned transcended both wit and humor; it is the sublime merriment of the Olympian divinities, the laugh evoked by Homer. Human beings, however, are not gods; when they laugh or when, as comic artists, they elicit laughter, it is by suggesting the permanent duality of man, "la puissance d'être à la fois soi et un autre" (". . . the ability to be at one and the same time oneself and another").[34]

Duality, the theme of the double, is one of the obsessions of Samuel Beckett's *oeuvre*. It is perhaps most vividly illustrated in another wordless work, his movie simply entitled *Film.*

Film is about perception: seeing and being seen. The protagonist is a man in flight; he flees from one eye in particular, the one that coincides with the camera. All eyes, however, terrify him, whether of human beings, animals, bird, fish, or those that might stare from reflective surfaces such as mirrors and windows. His efforts to escape the eye will suffer defeat. As Beckett writes in the introduction to his scenario: "Search of non-being in flight from extraneous perception breaking down in inescapability of self-perception" (p. 11).

Although we see mainly a single protagonist—with some extras—he is sundered into "object (O) and (E), the former in flight, the latter in pursuit" (p. 11). Beckett is also very clear about the angle that must be kept by the camera between E (itself until a final shot), and O, "an angle not exceeding 45 degrees" (p. 11). Twice E will exceed this "angle of immunity," and finally will do so deliberately, "when O is cornered" (p. 11).

Film begins outside, in the street. We are aware that the camera is searching for someone; it will be O. When he comes into view he is running along a dilapidated wall. His back is turned to the camera, the collar of his long, ill-fitting coat is turned up, and a silk scarf, held on his head by a battered hat, hides from view most of his hair and neck. Jostling a couple in his panic, O reaches a building that looks like a small factory but turns out to be his residence. On the stairs O, followed by an invisible E, will meet an old woman carrying a tray of fresh flowers tied by a string around her neck; she might be Flora and Pomona on the brink of dissolution. There is, however, a lovely smile on her lips before she meets the stare that makes her lose her sweet composure. Suddenly terror fills her old eyes, and she falls back in a swoon, or dead. The camera shows her lying at the bottom of the stairs, her flowers strewn over her lifeless form, a grotesque Ophelia. She has suffered what Beckett calls "the agony of perceivedness" (p. 16).

In the second volume of *Les Chemins de la Liberté, Le Sursis,* Jean-Paul Sartre describes vividly the discomfort of feeling that someone is watching him from the back. In a long, confessional letter written by the sadomasochist Daniel to his friend Mathieu, the professor of philosophy who is now on his way to the front, we find a detailed analysis of this sensation:

> Tu as certainement éprouvé, en métro, dans le foyer d'un théâtre, en wagon, l'impression soudaine et insupportable d'être épié par derrière. Tu te retournes mais déjà le curieux a plongé le nez dans son livre; tu ne peux pas arriver à savoir qui t'observait. Tu retournes à ta position première, mais tu sais que l'inconnu vient de relever les yeux, tu le sens à un léger fourmillement de tout ton dos, comparable à un resserrement violent et rapide de tous tes tissus. Eh bien, voilà ce que j'ai ressenti pour la première fois, le 26 septembre, à trois heures de l'après-midi, dans le parc de l'hôtel. Et il n'y avait personne. Entends-tu, Mathieu, personne. Mais le regard était là. . . . Depuis, je n'ai pas cessè d'être devant témoin. Devant témoin, même dans ma chambre close.

> (You must certainly have experienced in the subway, the train, a theater lobby, the sudden and unbearable sensation of being spied on from the back. You swing around but the inquisitive stranger has buried his nose in a book. There's no way of finding out who was staring at you. You resume your initial position, but you know that the stranger has just raised his eyes, and you feel by the quick, violent tension of your flesh that something is crawling up your back. I felt this for the first time on September twenty-six, at three P.M., in the hotel park. And there was no one there, Mathieu, do you hear, not a soul. . . . Since that day, I have not stopped being before a witness. There is always this witness, even when I'm in my room with the door shut.)[35]

Unlike Beckett's protagonist, Daniel derives a strange kind of joy from his discomfort, and finally even a reason for faith. In the light of the present discussion, however, it is curious to note that Sartre's "salaud" experiences the mixed emotions of laughter and terror. Echoing Pascal's "Pleurs, pleurs de joie!" he writes: "Pleurs de rire" ("Tears of laughter").[36] For Beckett, also, laughter and tears come to the same thing in the end.

The protagonist of *Film* is not alone in his room although we do not actually see E follow him in. Beckett writes: "They enter room together, E turning with O as he turns to lock the door behind him" (p. 22). The room is almost naked, holding little furniture but some life: a dog and a cat living in perfect harmony, a parrot in a cage, a goldfish in a bowl—all these creatures seem to stare at O. Even when the animals have been put out of the room—we laugh at the cat reentering as the dog is being put out, and vice versa, the parrot cage covered by the coat, the mirror draped by the rug which lay on the pallet, the curtains carefully drawn, the print with round, staring eyes (a Babylonian deity) ripped off the peeling wall, the fish bowl draped under the other half of the coat in order to avoid all eyes— there is not relief. As the protagonist sits down in a rocking chair at the center of the room, one senses that this man is not resting, that he is not at peace. With his hat still on, he appears to be a visitor, a transient guest in his own room. The chair itself is threatening; its headrest rising above the man's back has two apertures that look like hollow eye sockets. Even the folder, which contains family photographs to be examined one last time before the aged, wrinkled hands tear to shreds a whole existence, scattering it on the floor, is held shut by a string runing between two "eyes." Unbeknownst to the protagonist, E stands behind him, looking down over O's left shoulder.

O's psychopathic state reflects his instinctive awareness of that constant presence behind him. Like Sartre's Daniel he craves invisibility, and like Daniel he cannot achieve it. He will finally come face to face with himself, not in a mirror, but in the form of a real double. At the end of *Film* we will be shown the protagonist's face twice, as himself and as his facing other self. This is Beckett's description of E: "It is O's face (with patch) but with very different expression, impossible to describe, neither severity nor benignity, but rather acute *intentness*" (p. 47). It is the ultimate confrontation, between self and self.

Film was made with Buster Keaton, but the famous deadpan expression was not to be seen until the very end. Alan Schneider, the director of *Film,* writes in his published Notes: ". . . Buster, finally given the chance not only to let us see his face but to see him act, let loose from deep inside somewhere. When we finally saw it, that face paid off—even if we hadn't known it was Keaton's" (p. 88).

The presence at O's back was that of his double. Locked in his room he finds he cannot escape from that other self. The discovery is unbearable, and O brings his old hands up to his face, veiling his eyes, the one that sees, and the other covered by a patch. The seeing and the blind eye provide the perfect symbol for the divided self.

The image of the double suggests the duality which constitutes the essence of every creator, the man who is condemned to studying himself. Already in his early work on Proust, Beckett had written: "The artistic tendency is not expansive, but a contraction. And art is the apotheosis of solitude."[37] Finally what looks back at you is the work you have created.

Perhaps E is that work, looking with its steely, hawklike eye at its frightened, aging, dying maker. In a recent article, "Esthetic Judgment and the Comedy of Culture in Molière, Flaubert, and Beckett," Larry W. Riggs states the following about Beckett's work: "The problem of the self becomes the reader's or spectator's problem, as well as the writer's and the characters', because the nature and meaning of the thing that the former is reading or watching—and that is, therefore, the content of his own consciousness—are entirely problematical. Awareness of the play as play, or of the book as book, is metamorphosed by Beckett into awareness of *awareness* as such."[38] The work peruses the inner self. The final frame is a close-up of a single, uncovered eye.

Beckett's wordless plays are among his most eloquent works. They address us directly, reaching the very depths of our being. In them, as in the rest of Beckett's *oeuvre*, tragedy and comedy overlap, intertwine. These modern Harlequins and Pierrots gesture to us their puzzlement, their estrangement. Like Ionesco's orator at the end of *The Chairs*, they have no message, but something remains: the knowledge of the void.

Samuel Beckett's wordless plays are connected to the writer's earliest concerns as expressed in his 1929 essay, "Dante . . . Bruno . . . Vico . . . Joyce." From the start of his career as a writer and thinker Beckett addressed himself to the problem of rescuing language from excessive abstraction. He felt that English in particular had become dehydrated, deadened, "abstracted to death."[39] As Professor Sighle Kennedy argues in her thoroughly researched study, *Murphy's Bed*, Beckett was fascinated by Vico's theory "that all myths are based on prelingual gestures and concretion."[40] The implicit question is whether language could be made once again as concrete as gesture, that is, as the act of pointing mutely yet eloquently to the object one wishes to single out for attention. In his essay Beckett states: "In its first dumb form language was gesture. If a man wanted to say 'sea', he pointed to the sea."[41] Thus the young essayist seems to harken back to a time "when language consisted of gesture" and there was no difference between "the spoken and the written."[42]

Beckett admires Dante and Joyce for having created languages of their own making which approximated "the first 'sacred' stage"[43] of verbal expression as it might have arisen from the subterranean zone of prelingual perception. In her chapter, "Murphy's Mantic Language," Professor Kennedy explains with subtlety and accuracy how Beckett sought to undo the harm of mindless sound—increasingly abstract words—by weaving a literary text "whose words represent the signs of a primal silent force."[44] Indeed, Beckett points out that Dante constructed a synthetic language, a "vulgar" assembled from the purest elements of each regional dialect. Beckett stresses the fact that Dante "did not write in Florentine any more than in Neapolitan. He wrote a vulgar language that *could* have

68   *Rosette C. Lamont*

been spoken by an ideal Italian who had assimilated what was best in all the dialects of his country, but which in fact was certainly not spoken nor ever had been."[45] Thus, the language of the *Divine Comedy* was as strange to the Latin-reading elite of Dante's time as that of Joyce's *Work in Progress* was to its readers.

What made Joyce's language so bold and unusual was the fact that it was not written "only to be read."[46] Beckett makes much of Joyce's assumption that his text will be striking to the eye and ear, that it will be examined as one does a new and strange object and listened to. That is what lends it concreteness. Like Archibald Macleish's ideal poem which must "not mean but be," Joyce's poetic prose seems to perform a Dionysian dance. "The very words are tilted and effervescent," Beckett writes, concluding that Joyce's writing is not *about* something; *it is that something itself.*"[47]

By inventing an Indo-European Ur-tongue, Joyce "desophisticated"[48] the most dessicated of languages, English. Although *Murphy* testifies to the fact that Beckett could have followed in his predecessor's footsteps while achieving his own "mantic" expression, it became increasingly clear to him that the greatest temptation was that of stylistic brilliance, of being too *recherché*. Beckett turned to French not only because he had studied and taught it, or even because he was living in France, but for its foreignness, which placed him, as the user of this vehicle, in the position of wonder and estrangement with which primitive man regards the ambient world. By writing with utter directness and simplicity in this acquired tongue, Beckett invented for himself a form closer to meditation than to speech.

Yet even here there was room for misunderstanding, misinterpretation. Beckett's ideal was a language which would approximate silence. In his first novel, *Dream of Fair to Middling Women,* he says that "only the French language can give you the thing you want."[49] There the horizontal flow of text is constantly interrupted by "flints and pebbles."[50] These create accidents along the way, useful stops in the train of thought. The novel's antiheroic protagonist, Belacqua, speaks with admiration of "the incoherent continuum as expressed by . . . Rimbaud and Beethoven." He feels that their "audibilities are no more than punctuation in a statement of silences."[51]

Thus, from the very beginning Beckett aspired to an eloquent muteness. He wanted his words to be like a pointing finger. In this sense Beckett is profoundly mythical. He learned from Vico that "in Greek the fable was also called Mythos, myth, whence comes the Latin mutus, mute. For speech was born in mute times as mental (or sign) language which Strabo in a golden passage says existed before vocal or articulate language. . ."[52] Beckett's wordless dramaticules, television sketches, and his *Film* are fables for our time and for all times. By dispensing with words altogether,

Beckett has re-created on the stage, and on large and small screens, those "mute times" when man first started to question creation and his own role in it. His metaphysical clowns, like Rilke's acrobats, jump and fall as they stretch and reach. As we follow their doomed but noble efforts we rise with them above the wasteland of abstraction to the circumambient zone of universal myths.

Notes

1. Samuel Beckett, *Worstward Ho* (New York: Grove Press, 1983), p. 29.

2. David Bidney, "Myth, Symbolism and Truth," in *Myth and Literature, Contemporary Theory and Practice,* ed. John B. Vickery (Lincoln: University of Nebraska Press. 1966), p. 5.

3. Ibid., p. 11.

4. Ernst Cassirer, *Language and Myth,* trans. Suzanne K. Langer (New York: Dover 1946), p. 32.

5. Ibid., p. 43.

6. Bidney, p. 10.

7. Herbert Weisinger, "The Myth and Ritual Approach to Shakespearean Tragedy," in *Myth and Literature, Contemporary Theory and Practice,* p. 155.

8. Géza Róheim, "Myth and Folktale," in *Myth and Literature, Contemporary Theory and Practice,* p. 32.

9. Harold H. Watts, "Myth and Drama," in *Myth and Literature, Contemporary Theory and Practice,* p. 79.

10. Samuel Beckett, *Film,* Complete Scenario/Illustrations, Production shots with an essay, "On Directing *Film,*" by Alan Schneider (New York: Grove Press, 1969), p. 11. All subsequent references to *Film* are from this edition.

11. Samuel Beckett, *Waiting for Godot* (New York: Grove Press, 1954), p. 34. All subsequent references to *Waiting for Godot* are from this edition.

12. Samuel Beckett, *The Unnamable* (New York: Grove Press, 1958), p. 34.

13. From Stéphane Mallarmé's poem, "Le Tombeau d'Edgar Poe." The line reads: "Donner un sens plus pur aux mots de la tribu" ("to lend a purer meaning to the words of the tribe").

14. Samuel Beckett and Georges Duthuit, "Three Dialogues," in *Samuel Beckett,* ed. Martin Esslin (Englewood Cliffs, N. J.: Prentice Hall, 1965), p. 21.

15. Stéphane Mallarmé, "Le Genre ou des modernes," in *Crayonné au théâtre, Oeuvres Complètes* (Paris: Bibliothèque de la Pléiade, 1945), p. 319. This translation and all subsequent translations from the French are mine.

16. Mallarmé, "Autre étude de danse," p. 308.

17. Mallarmé, "Ballets,", p. 304.

18. Mallarmé, "Mimique," p. 310.

19. Ibid.

20. Ibid.

21. Robert F. Storey, *Pierrot, A Critical History of a Mask* (Princeton, N. J.: Princeton University Press, 1978), p. 113.

22. Mallarmé, "Notes sur le théâtre," p. 340.

23. "Gentlemen/Tramp" is the third chapter of Vivian Mercier's *Beckett/Beckett* (Oxford: Oxford University Press, paperback edition, 1979), p. 46.

24. "The Expulsed." This is the title of the first text in Samuel Beckett's *Nouvelles et textes pour rien* (Paris: Les Editions de Minuit, 1958).

25. Samuel Beckett, *Act Without Words I* in *Krapp's Last Tape and other dramatic pieces* (New York: Grove Press, 1980), p. 125. All subsequent references to *Act Without Words I* are to this edition.

26. Hugh Kenner, *Samuel Beckett, A Critical Study* (Berkeley and Los Angeles: University of California Press, 1973), p. 124.

27. *Act Without Words II* in *Krapp's Last Tape and other dramatic pieces,* p. 137. All subsequent references to *Act Without Words II* are to this edition.

28. From a personal, unpublished letter written by Samuel Beckett to the Polish Beckett critic and translator Antoni Libera.

29. Weisinger, p. 151.

30. Charles Baudelaire, "De l'essence du rire," *Curiosités Esthetiques, Oeuvres II* (Paris: Bibliothèque de la Pléiade, 1951), p. 179.

31. Samuel Beckett, *Malone meurt* (Paris: Less Editions de Minuit, 1951), p. 37. (*Malone Dies* [New York: Grove Press, 1956], p. 18).

32. Samuel Beckett, *Watt* (New York: Grove Press, 1959), p. 48.

33. Charles Baudelaire, *Less Fleurs du Mal, Oeuvres II* (Paris: Bibliothèque de la Pléiade, 1944), p. 175.

34. Ibid., p. 183.

35. Jean Paul Sartre, *Le Sursis* (Paris: Gallimard, 1945), p. 310.

36. Ibid., p. 317.

37. Samuel Beckett, *Proust* (New York: Grove Press, 1931), p. 47.

38. Larry W. Riggs, "Esthetic Judgment and the Comedy of Culture in Moliere, Flaubert, and Beckett," *The French Review,* vol. 54, no. 5 (April 1981), p. 688.

39. Samuel Beckett, "Dante . . . Bruno . . . Vico . . . Joyce," *Disjecta,* ed. Ruby Cohn (New York: Grove Press, 1984), p. 28.

40. Sighle Kennedy, *Murphy's Bed* (Lewisburg, Pa.: Bucknell University Press, 1971), p. 108.

41. Beckett, *Disjecta,* p. 24.

42. Ibid., p. 25.

43. Kennedy, p. 277.

44. Ibid., p. 295.

45. Beckett, *Disjecta,* p. 30.

46. Ibid., p. 27.

47. Ibid.

48. Ibid., p. 28.

49. Samuel Beckett, "Dream of Fair to Middling Women," *Disjecta,* p. 47.

50. Ibid.

51. Ibid., p. 48.

52. Giambattista Vico, *The New Science of Giambattista Vico,* trans. T. G. Bergin and M. H. Fisch (Ithaca: Cornell University Press, 1948), 2. 2. 1. 401. Quoted by Sighle Kennedy on p. 278 of *Murphy's Bed.*

STORYTELLING

Rites of Story

The Old Man at Play

Mary A. Doll

What is the sound of one hand clapping? This Zen koan with its unanswerable question jogs the mind out of a rationalistic habit of thought into true mindlessness. Who should know the rational habit of mind better than the old-man figure in Beckett's fiction and drama? Loving the old questions with their old answers, Beckett's old man has run the track of rationalism until its path has worn thin. Beckett shows that the track, like the old man himself, has come to the end of its line. Rationalism is the old ego, the old way, Winnie's classics, or the track "A" takes in *That Time,* bringing him "in the end to the station . . . all closed down and boarded up Doric terminus of the Great Southern and Eastern all closed down and the colonnade crumbling away so what next" (TT, p. 33).[1]

At the end, when all else fails, the old man tells himself stories. "What I need now is stories," says Molloy (TN, p. 13); "It's storytime, where was I?" intones Hamm (E, p. 48); Krapp listens to his opus, really the story of his shadow self; and in *Ohio Impromptu* Reader and Listener, each other's Other, read to and listen from the open pages of the book of their life. Story, however, does not follow the sequence of lived time; refusing forward movement, it contains little plot and less chronology. Rather, it interrupts a rational habit of mind, breaking tracked patterns of literal responses and logical assumptions. Accordingly, the old man is drawn into story not so much to *tell* as to *listen to* words. But what do words say when there is nothing left to tell?

Word-saying, indeed, comprises the heart of the dramatic situation in Beckett's drama. While storytelling, a familiar motif in Beckettian fiction, has been the subject of the critical writings of Judith Dearlove, Ted Estess, Bruce Kawin, and James Hanford (among others),[2] it is the drama that turns telling into a listening act. As a type or kind, the old man typically needs to put the facts of his life on stage so that he can play-act with them. Other features of his being make him immediately recognizable to an audience. He wears, typically, a long black coat or dressing gown, is bowed down with pain or fatigue, and has an extraordinary head. Either he has something wrong with his head (like Henry in *Embers*), or he has a heart in his head (like Hamm in *Endgame*), or the hair on his head has grown so long that, as Stan Gontarski suggests, "it seems to have grown for years beyond death."[3] Clearly, the head signifies not a thinking place, but a place in which and through which story's words "sound," connecting present and past, life and death.

With this archetypal old man and his ritual story, Beckett achieves a wonderfully poetic, dramatic occasion, the basic building block of which is repetition: repetitive character, repetitive words, repetitive actions, repetitive scenes. Mircea Eliade, in his work on ritual, describes repetition in ways that relate strikingly with Beckett's drama of the storytelling old man. According to Eliade certain dance and song rites satisfy a basic human need to return to the roots of Being. Repetitious movement and repeated syllables provide the means by which a celebrant can propel him or herself out of "this time" into a more mythical "that time," *in illo tempore*. As Eliade writes, "Sacred time appears under the paradoxical aspect of circular time, reversible and recoverable, a sort of eternal mythical present time that is periodically reintegrated by means of rites."[4] In story the old man of Beckett's drama engages in just such a ritual recovery of Being that, once felt, must forever be renewed.

Three moments identify three turning points in storytelling, making the old man's obsessive need an act of profound ritual importance. The first moment is Regression. The old man can't get certain words out of his head—"stone" and "ruin," for instance. The story he tells himself revolves around his words literally and figuratively, circling over them in maddening repetition. As an audience sees him pacing circles and hears him resaying his words, a dance of meanings combines language, action, and consciousness. Drama becomes a pulling-in and a pulling-down to where story's words are heard mindlessly, as in a koan. Clearly, the words to which the self responds must empty of conceptual meaning. The old man thus uses his head not as a place for figuring *out* meaning, but as a place where meaning takes on the shape of figures, *within*.

A second key moment in the rite of storytelling is Encounter. Words, emptied of precise denotation by an act of eternal (infernal) repetition, evoke other presences. Figures, ghosts, images, memories—drawn up from the deep past—throw the old man back to where he can touch repressed pain. There, on the fields of imagination, language releases its "presential" power that hovers around the various connotations of spoken meaning. Inside and among such presences, an old man's personal hell can transpose into a mythical Hades. But unlike the encounters of mythic heroes, Beckett's old-man encounters are nonheroic, weakening rather than strengthening ego and all the ego controls.

A third moment seldom reached in the early drama and only fleetingly reached in recent plays is the ritual moment of Reawakening. The old man's story, not just *his* "to tell," transposes into *its* "to listen to." Like a celebrant, the old man mediates two times—one sacred, the other profane—where a deeper dimension of Being lives of itself. In Jungian terms this coming-to-life of soul, or anima, shares an affinity with animals and feels like a flame. Jung says, "It is something that lives of itself, that makes us live; it is a life behind consciousness."[5] Jung's definition of soul as a deeper, lower livingness relates suggestively to Beckett's definition of language as "extra-audenary" (D, p. 293), evoking the unsaid by the said (L); or of memory as "explosive," choosing *its* own time and place for the performance of *its* miracle (P, pp. 20–21, emphasis mine). When, thus, the old man experiences Reawakening, he is feeling the basic building blocks of story ("stone," "ruin") in new ways that allow him to touch, not just to think about, the foundations of his pain.

The old man's ritualistic need to tell stories has consistently occupied Beckett's dramatic writings. Three plays, covering three decades, demonstrate this consistency in ritual storytelling and reveal as well Beckett's use of stage as a place of potential dramatic transformation. *Endgame* (1958), *That Time* (1976), and *Ohio Impromptu* (1981) all chart an absolute necessity of the storytelling act for the discovery of the source of Being. But the plays also illustrate Beckettian theater as uniquely integrative: action on one stage transforming action to another; audience acting with actor, becoming actor. Actors and audience alike must listen, listen, in a never-ending need to hear the words better. As the same words are sounded repeatedly in new combinations, the actor's head empties and fills—like tides of the sea. What becomes dramatic is not physical action and grand gesture—out there—but internal leaps of imagination, in the active imaginations of both audience and actor.[6]

The original stage design of *Endgame,* by Jacques Noel, suggests this dramatic quality of enacted saying, its effect on consciousness. The stage, looked at from the audience, appears like a vast empty skull, with windows like eye sockets. As the characters wheel about the center, emptiness begins to acquire depth, and seeing acquires a listening dimension. With such emphasis on the head, emptied, the audience must begin to function differently in the head. Faced with such games at the end, in *Endgame,* viewers in the audience must begin to create new meanings inside their own skulls.

With a toque on his head like a hollow crown, Hamm resembles an old king defending his hollow ways. Similar to his predecessors, Krapp, Henry, Pozzo, or Malone (from the fiction), Hamm—the archetypal Old Man—carries the sense of an old ego into our modern world. Immobilized, face covered with a large blood-stained handkerchief, body draped with a sheet, he also reincarnates the figure in "Echo's Bones," about to set sail over the waters. These multiple associations converge to suggest that dying to the old order, the old ego, the old way—*that* dying—is the great project of rebirth.

Hamm's oldness points to pivotal change in two distinct ways. First, his decrepitude is such that his body fills with holes. He is a sieve, plagued by constant leakage. Blind, he has a hole in his heart and a gaping hole in his head, for which he requires a painkiller. "There's something dripping in my head," he says (p. 18). Were it not for these holes, however, it would be impossible for another order of reality to seep through. The holes "crack" consciousness. Secondly, Hamm's language, a mix of literalism and fantasy, suggests his affinity with border situations. While he loves the comfort that an interpreted world can bring—the old questions, the old answers—he also has a fertile imagination. He thinks of the "beyond" as a place of green hills (p. 39), and he remembers, with yearning, flowers in the field (p. 42) and rising corn (p. 44). When pushed to his limits with nowhere to go, Hamm goes back to his story. Through story he allows the fields of memory to fertilize his imagination.

The Unnamable referred to story as "incomprehensibly mine" (TN, p. 413), where a storyteller can "be again." In accord with the original meaning of the word "reconciliation"—to return, to refind origins—storytelling accomplishes a fundamentally regressive act. The return takes one back to what lies on the other side of forgetfulness: first, or primal memories. In myth the Other side, the Underworld, has its own topography of fields and corn, known as the Elysian Fields that bloom in death. When, therefore, Hamm goes back to story, he begins a regression to something very deep and very primal inside himself.

The story setting, which emphasizes oldness, prepares an auditor to hear with the ears of a child. We are taken back to an early-old time when familiar ideas, stripped of old meanings, stand forth anew—as images. The setting, a deserted hole, both mirrors and deepens the stage setting, giving emptiness a depth of metaphoric image. The heart of the story, of course, concerns an early moment in Hamm's life as a child; but against the setting in imaginary time, lived facts metamorphose. Concerning a feudal lord to whom paupers must make petition, the story enables Hamm to exercise power over the kingdom of his mind. It appears that one pauper, from a "hole" far away and uninhabited, now seeks aid for his child. Hamm, as lordly narrator, enjoys the role he gives himself in story and demonstrates distance from its situation of need by ridiculous verbal embellishments: "It was a glorious day, I remember"; "It was an extraordinarily bitter day, I remember"; "It was a howling wild day, I remember." Clearly, Hamm only playacts and merely exercises word skills; true memory has not yet been engaged. Why such circumlocution? In moving around the moment of Encounter, circling it with evasion and cleverness, Hamm forstalls memory's truth.

But not even the winds of rhetoric can destroy the breath of spirit. The pauper's petitioning question, which concerns the child, sharpens that point at which "telling" and "listening" converge. Drained by the efforts of bombast, Hamm in the midst of his own story makes ready to hear its question on more than one level. He indicates this shift in consciousness by employing images of the sea: "I don't know. *(Pause.)* I feel rather drained. *(Pause.)* The prolonged creative effort. *(Pause.)* If I could drag myself down to the sea! I'd make a pillow of sand for my head and the tide would come in" (p. 61). Letting tides fill his head signals a moment in story when Hamm's roleplaying breaks down so that, ceasing to play the role of tyrant, he can become petitioner; ceasing to be the teller, he can become the told. Hamm readies himself for an encounter with the question: Would he consent to take in the child?

For Hamm to "take in the child" would be for him to regress back in time to the feeling of the child when he, like the pauper's son in the story, had been abandoned by his father; when he, like his namesake, had inherited the curse of the Father. It would be a supreme test of willed superiority and ego control to return to the source of pain. For, once, Hamm had indeed cried in the night and in darkness and had, once, received no answer from his father. Rather than literalizing the situation of his past, Hamm needs to fantasize its terror, returning the moment *now* to the fields of imaginative power *then,* until power and its opposite terror can change, shift, soften, metamorphose, create. If Hamm can bring himself to the brink of story's question—would he consent to take in the child—he could punch holes in his literal tendency to call story a "chronicle," the events of *this* time, only.

Endgame, an example of an aborted fiction with drama, never quite gets inside its dramatic situation. Concluding his story, Hamm says, "Well, there we are, there I am, that's enough" (p. 83). "Enough," apparently, is simple telling, when the *I* and the *me* never meet. At the end, Hamm covers his face with his handkerchief, recalling the suffering Christ; but psychic wounds have not sufficiently crucified imagination to allow holes of pain to seep like the sea into memory. Instead, holes are covered so as to staunch the flow of suffering: "Old stauncher!" Hamm says at the end, "*(Pause.)* You . . . remain" (p. 84).

That Time, an even more aborted story, fragments time by splitting it off among three voices, speaking at the mercy of their memories. Katharine Worth made an important point about the play when she distinguished it not as "situation" but as "the sense of" situation: drama coming through sound and sensing.[7] Interestingly, to the degree that it tells fewer chronicled events, drama intensifies. As storytelling becomes more impossible to "perform," performance becomes more and more a listening-to, turning listening into action and action into listening. Beckett intends this shift in emphasis in his play by a stage setting that displays a face "floating in its white hair" in the middle of stage darkness, addressed by a voice from three different time periods and coming from three different stage locations. "A," "B," and "C," the three speakers, together with the listening self called Listener, form four distinct aspects of selfhood: youth, midlife, maturity, old age. The white-haired old man presents an image of the wiseman figure of fairytale or myth, or perhaps an ancient sage of the East, Lao-Tse or Confucius. But the anguish and apparent lack of comprehension on the old man's part suggest that wisdom can no longer be "told" or even narrated; it must be petitioned.

The voice of "A" tells of a time, "that time," when a child's loneliness seems like a dry hell among old ruins and sharp nettles. This moment echoes another drama, *Endgame*. Like the pauper's "hole," this place of the child's abandonment is empty, not at all a part of the living. Also, like *Endgame*'s "situation at Kov" (p. 52), an extreme solitary nature creates the condition out of which fantasy is born. "A" learns make believe "talking to yourself who else loud imaginary conversation . . . on a stone among the giant nettles making it up now one voice now another" (p. 31). In addition, "A" speaks "Imaginary conversation," carrying on dialogues with other, earlier selves. But here images of sharpness—the nettle and the stone—give loneliness texture, even *place,* suggesting that the child's extreme condition has its own dimension, its own boundary of significance.

"A's" voice resounds with that of "C," both voices relating a time, "that time," of desolation in maturity. "C's" hell is not so much a matter of being without humankind as it is being in the midst of others with whom one has no contact whatsoever: "eyes passing over you and through you like so much thin air" (p. 36). The voice of "C" tells of an incessant quest to find touchstones between the self and culture. But the civilized institutions of culture, erected as foundations of external communication, provide no nourishment. Art galleries, churches, post offices, museums: "C" searches them all for validation that he is a real part of the mainstream. Only when he catches a glimpse of a face behind a glass in a picture gallery does he sense himself. This tiny moment reveals an enormous point. What holds the eye and fires the soul has nothing to do with the great works of famous people; what inspires the soul is simply an Other's flicker onto your consciousness: "till you hoisted your head and there before your eyes when they opened a vast oil black with age and dirt someone famous in his time some famous man or woman or even child . . . where gradually as you peered trying to make it out gradually of all things a face appeared . . ." (p. 30).

"B," in the second stage of life, achieves a Return to an earlier place of Being, where love and possibility teeter on the edge. The image-clusters of

"B's" story circle around the word "stone," mentioned four times and a fifth time in combination.

> on the stage together in the sun on the stone at the edge of the little wood and as far as the eye could see the wheat turning yellow vowing every now and then you loved each other just a murmur not touching or anything of that nature you one end of the stone she the other long low stone like millstone. (P. 29)

If, like Dante's quester, "B" can get beyond the hell of "that time," he must imagine the moment differently. He must acquire an imagination of stone, feeling its sharp hardness as a cold part of himself that has petrified his ability to respond. Jung once said, "The making of the stone is woman's work and child's play."[8] By connecting the stone with the old man, Beckett might be implying a connection of the old man with his opposites, the child and the Feminine. This implication is borne out with the word "stone," which is anything but fixed in literal definition. It shifts according to what other word groups combine with it. Refusing single meaning, "stone" takes on doubleness, both as a place where being-alone is being-together-with and as a place where togetherness is lonesome. "B's" stone thus mediates the stone of "A" and "C," uniting their separate fragments as two parts of a whole. Similarly, although in the storied fragment no touching or speaking occurs, the stone cements feeling. Even "millstone" continues this implicit doubleness; it carries the poetic vehicle both of what weights "B" down with mental burden, like millstone, and also of what grinds feeling: "wheat turning yellow," chaff to grain, like millstone. If "B" were to weigh his burdens differently, more imaginatively, he just might be able to see the grains of story's truth. Surely, "B's" stone, like the philosopher's stone, contains a poetry of oppositions!

Another of "B's" fragments in the ritual of storytelling connects "stone" with water—its natural opposite:

> alone on the end of the stone with the wheat and blue or the towpath alone on the towpath with the ghosts of the mules the drowned rat or bird or whatever it was floating off into the sunset. (P. 35)

"B's" story regresses further back in memory to an image of himself alone with his lover. On a literal level the image of death and desertion suggests closure of "B's" love, a world collapsed. On another level, however, dying produces multiplicity, fluidity, animation. Alone, "B" metaphorically accompanies ghosts. He shares his personal hell with bulky shapes that come before him in animal forms: mules, a rat, a bird. In listening, one hears more than a fragment of plot; one hears how "the blues" transcribe like a barge a mule pulls along the waters of a canal.

"B's" story moves from the edge of a little wood to a towpath and from land to sea. Precisely because "B's" animal images are not empirical, real animals, they drag the soul.

"B's" final image cluster pushes Listener even farther back toward an encounter with self, where images animate deep consciousness. Darkness takes on density, enabling one to see into shades of meaning, and to hear words ring:

> that time in the end when you tried and couldn't by the window in the dark and the owl flown to hoot at someone else or back with a shrew to its hollow tree and not another sound hour after hour hour after hour not a sound. (P. 37)

This image deals directly with hollow space and its potential for fullness. Silence surrounds each word, not as "mere" silence, but as the sound of "no sound." Equally, darkness is not the absence of light, but the presence of another universe. For Beckett's poetics, night activates soul and requires thereby sharper seeing and shrewder hearing to sense its ways. In his "Peintres de l'empêchement" Beckett speaks to this point, describing true seeing as an acquired skill of night vision: "on commence enfin à voir, dans le noir. Dans le noir qui est aube et midi et soir et nuit d'un ciel vide, d'une terre fixe" ("One begins at last to see, in the night. In the night which is dawn and noon and evening and night in a blank sky, in a still land," (my translation) (p. 6).[9] In the final fragment of "B's" story this suggests a need for Listener to awaken not to dawn but to *night's* dawn and to the dawning "sense" that night-life creates.

Sensed thus, Listener could "hear" inside "B's" final image cluster the hollow spaces of his mind coming alive in animal fashion. Owl and shrew go together into the hollow space of a tree. An owl, wise in the head, keen with the eyes, asleep during the day, comes alive at night. It takes a shrew to its hollow tree, leaving us to imagine a deadly scene: owl feeding upon shrew. But together, owl and shrew form a composite of the senses; a shrew, blind of eye and awake in day, senses with its nose—smelling at every corner. In one way we can imagine a primal rite, but in another way we can imagine two sensory ways of Being coming together, wisely, shrewdly, with clear vision and keen hearing. In such a dying, we can imagine fierce livingness, where the senses digest as never before!

Feeling words, like hearing them, empowers the rites of story to Reawaken sense. A story begins, after all, with a simple image: man on a stone at the edge of a wood. We have sensed that stone in many ways: *seeing* its connection with the old man's literalism and obsessiveness, *feeling* a difficulty in its comprehension—even *hearing* it. For it is the sounding of the "o" sound in "stone" re-sounding in the "no sound" of the final fragment that strikes the real chord of depth, the basic words of

"B's" story: "no," "stone," "low," towpath," "float," "ghost," "old," "flown." Out of such deep musical tones comes a flowing of sound that creates worlds of meaning. The stone as millstone also implies stone as grindstone, or brimstone, multiplying senses, until sound becomes a true touchstone of the self.

Finally, *Ohio Impromptu*, a recent minimalist drama, maximizes sound, drawing attention even further into the listening rather than the telling act. As in *That Time* a character (called Listener) listens, but here Listener assumes a more active role, knocking with his left hand at key moments in Reader's narration. Knocking seems to accomplish two purposes: to interrupt the flow of the story's text (preventing, thereby, Reader from overlooking phrases of importance, forcing Reader to re-read), and to allow proper pause between phrases. Listener, with his corrective knocks to consciousness, insists on spaces around words—proper empty spacing—so that the words may empty and fill with meaning. And the left hand does the knocking, for Listener's left side of intuition is in need of hearing words more keenly, less sequentially.[10] Listening requires a shrewd ear, for, when "Nothing is left to tell" (p. 34), one must listen to what is "left."

Another room, another window, another sense of *in extremis* ties the dramatic situation of *Ohio Impromptu* to *That Time*. A past memory of the "dear one" and unspoken words haunt present time. Other ties to *Embers*, a radio play of the fifties, describe an old man's torture as "Nothing, all day nothing. *(Pause.)* All night nothing. *(Pause.)* Not a sound" (p. 121). In *Embers* Henry walks incessantly along the edge of the sea, alone, "just to be with me," and in being-with continues his unfinished story of Bolton and Holloway. As with the text-within-a-text of Reader and Listener, Henry's story within a story recounts a man who tells stories: "Stories, stories, years and years of stories, till the need came on me, for someone, to be with me, anyone, a stranger, to talk to, imagine he hears me" (p. 100). Storytelling does not allay the pain of Henry's world but only makes that pain keener: "Fire out, bitter cold, white world, great trouble, not a sound" (p. 119). And, like Listener's knocks on the white deal table shared by Reader in *Ohio Impromptu*, hard sounds punctuate the soundlessness of this white world: Henry's walking "boots on shingle" (p. 95), horses' hooves walking "on hard road" (p. 104), and the music master's "blow of ruler on piano case" (p. 107). It is as if hearing what is "left" demands sharp knocks to the ear, in the manner of the Zen master striking blows between the shoulders during zazen.

The nightside of the old man's life in *Ohio Impromptu*, his terror, is described by Reader's text as follows:

In this extremity his old terror of night laid hold of him again. After so long a lapse that as if never been. *(Pause. Looks closer.)* Yes, after so long a lapse that as if never been. Now with redoubled force the fearful symptoms described at length page forty paragraph four . . . White nights now again his portion. (P. 31)

"Terror" and "fear" rather than "torture" and "anguish" suggest that an old man's pain has taken yet another turn. Reader seems at a loss to comprehend the words he reads, even though the text is his. Comprehension, the act of grasping ideas, utterly lacks function here. What, then, has caused the old man's nights to "come alive" with such vividness, in the absence of rational understanding?

Words, Metaphors, Images. Sound. These build blocks of sensing—not "common" sense. When the senses reawaken, words fill and flow, becoming so much more than the thing signified. Reader's text pushes comprehension back from the "little" left to tell to the "nothing" left to tell, "where nothing ever shared" (p. 30). The text forces Reader off the rock of literalism, nothing as "no thing," and washes his senses with new hearing. "Nothing ever" activates sharing, turning at the negative to a positive "ever shared"—forever *sharing* nothingness.

In the next "extra-audenary" passage, metaphor, sound, and sense converge around a description of the sea:

At the tip he would always pause to dwell on the receding stream. How in joyous eddies its two arms conflowed and flowed united on. Then turn and his slow steps retrace. (P. 29)

We set sail to this place in story, on the receding stream, where he would "dwell." He is, inside the text at the moment of story's Regression, back, in, and on the empty dwelling place. Similarly, water has a dwelling or living quality, with its joyous eddies and arms that seem to embrace and give comfort. No wonder the old man thinks deeply, dwelling on an image that, of itself, can turn pain to joy! So, too, does sound soften the mournful "o." Unlike *That Time*'s repetitive circling of "o," here a full range of vowel sounds plays within meaning. As in the title, *Ohio Impromptu,* sound opens away from the long "o" in "Ohio" to other vowels in "Impromptu," seeming to play with and thereby create new meanings. Indeed, the words of this passage—descriptive of the sea as picture—also are descriptive of the sea as sound, moving in a flowing way back and forth in assonance between and among the letters. Dwelling on this passage, one's mind dips to new depths, other worlds, different senses.

The moment of Encounter brings the Return back to where past fills with "presence." In *Ohio Impromptu* the storied phrase "One night" signals an encountering moment when, much like "Once upon a time," then and now come together briefly and poetically:

One night as he sat trembling head in hands from head to foot a man appeared to him and said, I have been sent by—and he named the dear name—to comfort you. (P. 32)

Traditionally, the Night Visitor symbolizes consciousness reawakening in dream. Beast reawakens Beauty to her two-sided nature, for instance, as Eros does Psyche. Here the Night Visitor revivifies *multiple* presences of figures from inside the old man's stories told over time. Here the Night Visitor recalls Holloway in Henry's text, sent to relieve Bolton's pain, or the "shade" in Reader's text, or Listener in *Ohio Impromptu*, or the psalmist's text. It becomes all of these, and more. Beckett's stories force an encounter with text, where drama "plays" one text over and against another, contextually, continually.

Encounter as text-encounter draws attention to a dramatic potential of language itself. Beckett seems to take Saussure's *langue/parole* distinction even farther, however. He seems to dramatize language as *music,* in the manner of what George Steiner wrote—namely, that language "passes into music" when it attains a "maximal intensity of its being."[11] The word "Impromptu" as a musical term and the Encountering moment heard as a "Second Movement" bear out these musical notions.[12] Then too, language presents itself, becomes presential, presenting "presence." This theory of language relates to Philip Wheelwright's *Metaphor and Reality,* wherein he makes reference to early man's experience of the world as a continual, hovering "presence."[13]

Metaphor coming alive to preliterate literalism! Two expressionless men "as alike in appearance as possible" face each other without speaking. "So the sad tale a last time told they sat on as though turned to stone" (p. 34). Vowels play sound among consonants, softly—almost sweetly—while the two give a stoney image. "No sound. So sat on as though turned to stone." Words repeat. The old man's stories repeat too, like stones of a past. But here in *Ohio Impromptu* stone and old man unite. Turning to stone, the old man *becomes* stone: unblinking, expressionless, nonhearing, nonseeing, mindless. "To sound of reawakening. What thought who knows what profounds of mind. Of mindlessness. Wither no light can reach. No sound" (p. 34). Circling around and around the same material—endlessly—words grind text, wear it down (the volume is "worn"), softening meaning, until chaff becomes grain, stone mills stone, and mind reawakens to true mindlessness.

What do words say when there is nothing left to tell? *Ohio Impromptu* transcribes a koan to the drama of a stage where nothing is encountered. Beckett's old man never succeeds, as traditional mythical heroes do, with successful dragon battles and boon retrievals. We have moved off the stage of "thing"ness. Rather, Beckett's ritual of storytelling accomplishes a much more difficult task. From *Endgame* through *That Time* to the recent minimalist work, the old man has strained his ears. His task is to be "holy"—fully present; not "to tell," but to "listen," until his petrified concepts turn to fancy.[14]

Notes

In citing Beckett's works in the notes the following abbreviations have been used and all references will be to these editions:

D. "Denis Devlin" (Review), *transition* (April–May 1938): 289–94.

E. *Endgame,* Translated by the author (New York: Grove Press, 1958).

EB. "Echo's Bones," in *Collecied Poems in French and English* (New York: Grove Press, 1961).

Emb. *Embers* in *Krapp's Last Tape and Other Dramatic Pieces* (New York: Grove Press, 1960)

L. Letter to Axel Kaun (September 1937).

OI. *Ohio Impromptu* in *Rockaby and Other Short Pieces* (New York: Grove Press, 1981).

P. *Proust* (New York: Grove Press, 1931).

Pein. "Peintres de l'empêchement," *Derriere le mirror* (June 1948): 3–7.

TN. *Three Novels by Samuel Beckett* (New York: Grove Press, 1976).

TT. *That Time* in *Ends and Odds* (New York: Grove Press, 1974–76).

1. For this and all subsequent references to works by Beckett see the list of abbreviations above.

2. See, for instance, Judith E. Dearlove, "The Voice and Its Words," *Journal of Beckett Studies* 3 (Summer 1978): 56–75; Ted Estess, "The Inenarrable Contraption: Reflections on the Metaphor of Story," *Journal of American Academy of Religion* 42: 3 (September 1974): 415–34; Bruce Kawin, *Telling It Again and Again: Repetition in Literature and Film* (Ithaca: Cornell University Press, 1972); and James Hansford, "Seeing and Saying in *As the Story was Told,*" *Jounal of Beckett Studies* 8 (Autumn 1982): 75–94.

3. S. E. Gontarski, "The World Premiere of *Ohio Impromptu,*" *Journal of Beckett Studies* 8 (Autumn 1982): 135.

4. Mircea Eliade, *The Sacred and the Profane: The Nature of Religion,* trans. Willard R. Trask (New York: Harper, 1961), p. 70.

5. C. G. Jung, "Archetypes of the Collective Unconscious," in *Archetypes and the Collective Unconscious,* trans. R. F. C. Hull (Princeton: Princeton University Press, 1977), pp. 26–27.

6. The imagination, and notably the head—as "seat of consciousness" where imaginary leaps can take place—is discussed by Jung in his work with hermetic symbols in his *Alchemical Studies* (Princeton: Princeton University Press, 1968), pp. 72, 80, 240 ff.

7. Katharine Worth, "Beckett's Fine Shades," *Journal of Beckett Studies* 1 (1976): 76.

8. Quoted in A. Vitale, "Saturn: The Transformation of the Father," in *Fathers and Mothers* (New York: Spring Publications, 1974), p. 27.

9. Night seeing, thus, renders darkness with its own natural setting, totally unrelated to either negatives or pessimism.

10. For more on the significance of the "left" side of Beckett's characters, particularly his women, see my "The Demeter Myth in Beckett," *Journal of Beckett Studies* 11 (forthcoming).

11. George Steiner, *Language and Silence: Essays on Language, Literature and Film* (New York: Atheneum Press, 1967), p. 42.

12. Gontarski, p. 133.

13. Philip Wheelwright, *Metaphor and Reality* (Bloomington: Indiana University Press, 1968), pp. 134–35.

14. The word "fancy" is not associated with the old-man characters but rather with the female characters of the recent plays, in *Footfalls* most notably. The old man's words may be different, but the use of the head as a fantasy place, full of fancy, and in stark contrast to a grim, lived reality, provides a powerful means of connecting the two.

Liminality

An Approach to Artistic Process in Endgame

Susan Maughlin

"Something is taking its course" is the singular reply Clov gives to Hamm's anguished question, "What's happening, what's happening?"[1] Although Clov's reply is devoid of specifics and is so vague as to seem pointless, it nonetheless smacks true. A paradox of vagueness and rightness, the line is an emphatic statement acknowledging and embodying the unnamed: it shows but does not clarify. It also describes precisely the action of the play—something takes its course. Change occurs in *Endgame,* simultaneously stealthy and blatant, seeming both impossible and inevitable, but the hows and whys of it are left unsaid; it is silent testimony to the power of that which is sensed but not articulated. The play's sparseness provokes a rich metaphorical quality, inciting a multiplicity of interpretations. I would like to explore a reading in which what takes its course is the inevitable unfolding and the seemingly impossible coalescence of the creative process. In this model, Hamm is author and Clov is character. Through their interaction, Beckett shows—but does not explain—artistic process.

In *The Shape of Chaos,* a study of the art of Samuel Beckett, David Hesla briefly mentions the author/character metaphor as one of several interpretations to be discerned in *Endgame*. He describes Hamm as a writer of declining power pushed nonetheless to the act of expression. Clov is a reticent character who becomes unavailable to Hamm in the end.[2] Victor Turner's notions of liminality and change can here serve as a tool for a much fuller development of this metaphor, showing in detail the relation between Hamm and Clov, author and character, as they interact and affect each other, working toward maturity.

Victor Turner describes liminality as a stage of transition and change in which paradox is created to expose the "building blocks" of a culture. The author/character metaphor shows the building blocks of an act of forming, the components of Hamm's "prolonged creative effort" (p. 61), and we may thus expose and discern them at the height of their strangeness and with all their illogical power. Turner himself draws a connection between liminality and creativity:

Genuine creative imagination, inventiveness, or inspiration goes beyond spatial imagination or any skill in forming metaphors. It does not necessarily associate visual images with given concepts and proportions. Creative imagination is far richer than imagery; it does not consist in the ability to evoke sense impressions and it is not restricted to filling gaps in the map supplied by perceptions. It is called "creative" because it is the ability to create concepts and conceptual systems that may correspond to nothing in the senses (even though they may correspond to something in reality), and also because it gives rise to unconventional ideas. This is the very creative darkness of liminality, that lays hold of the basic forms of life. These are more than logical structures.[3]

Examining the "creative darkness of liminality" will enable us to better understand the creative darkness of *Endgame*.

Turner first used the concept of liminality in his study of the Ndembu tribe of Southcentral Africa. The term was originally used by Belgian folklorist Arnold Van Gennep in his study of rites of passage, where he detected a three-part structure: separation, margin or limen, and reaggregation. The intermediate section is what interests Turner. He defines limen as a threshold, but in rites of passage it is very often a long threshold, more like a tunnel; the state of being on the threshold or in the tunnel is "liminality," and those undergoing the process are "liminaries."[4] In the Ndembu rituals he studied, every article, ritual element, gesture, song, or unit of space and time stood for something other than itself, serving a symbolic function of which the Ndembu were aware. Their term for a ritual element literally meant both landmark or beacon, and blaze, as in blazing a trail.[5] This is a paradoxical combination of a single-unit, self-defined element (landmark or beacon), and a series of undifferentiated elements (blaze) acquiring meaning solely through their relationship to each other. A blaze is a physical chain of markings enabling one to venture into the unknown, unfamiliar, and hence dangerous, territory and find the way back again. In Ndembu rites, the use is metaphorical, and metaphor is a way of applying the known qualities of one thing to something else which looms unknown.

Metaphor is therefore a tool of ritual:

The important thing for those who use metaphorical means is to build up as elaborately as they may a structure of ideas, embodied in symbols, and a structure of social positions, symbolically expressed, which will keep chaos at bay and create a mapped area of security.[6]

Keeping chaos manageable is one task of society. Although the subject of *Endgame* may well be the unmanageability of chaos, the play itself serves as a blazed trail, taking the audience into a bizarre land and back out again. We may well change along the way; if we are not safer, then we are more familiar with our unsafeness—our self-consciousness is part of the liminal territory.

It is Turner's premise that cultures set up a dialogue between periods of structure and periods of anti-structure. He associates structure with conservation of the culture, and anti-structure, or liminality, with transition points and growth. In Ndembu culture, liminality is not a spontaneous occurrence, but a carefully planned stage in the rites dealing with major life-changes such as birth, death, adulthood, and marriage; the stage is designed to reveal the "true" meaning of the culture's sacraments. Hence by studying mid-transitional states of liminality, according to Turner, one can find the "building blocks" and "root paradigms" of the culture: "The components of what I have called anti-structure, such as communitas and liminality, are the conditions for the production of root metaphors."[7]

To see how such building blocks are exposed, it is necessary to take a look at the tripartite structure of liminality. It consists of overlapping phases of grinding down and reconstruction, with a midpoint area characterized by paradox. There is frequent use of symbolism of opposites: the Ndembu might use a hut to represent both a womb and a tomb, with nakedness alluding to the newly born and to the dead. Sacramental symbols break apart and rearrange; proportion and context change, isolating and emphasizing various features, thereby throwing their meaning into relief. Paradox resonates by odd juxtaposition, generating strangeness and absurdity. In his laudatory criticism of friend and painter Henri Hayden, Beckett himself expresses the same notion: "Everything is recognizable, but not to be known. Strange order of things made from an order lacking objects, from objects with order."[8] We can say the same of *Endgame*.

The grinding-down portion of liminality refers to the breaking up of the identity of the initiate's previous status with its conventional classifications. Liminaries undergo physical hardship, exposure to harsh weather, ridicule, and humiliation, and they are subjected to unanswerable riddles. The purpose is to reduce them to dust or malleable clay to enable their new or elevated status to be impressed upon them by their culture. Liminaries form deep bonds with each other, a kind of ultimate sense of community that Turner labels "communitas." Silence often characterizes liminality, as well as complete obedience by the liminaries to authority. As the reconstruction portion is folded into the rite, richly ambiguous symbols and elements of the fantastic are introduced. Masks and monsters are prevalent. Turner sees this as a primordial mode of abstraction; cultural wholes are broken down into parts, the parts isolated and rearranged to be experienced and examined, and finally regenerated into new, suitable combinations. In Ndembu society, this process is firmly controlled by those in positions of authority.

We no longer live in a tribal society and, consequently, matters are different today. Turner coined the term "liminoid" to describe the secular, contemporary version of the liminal:

> The "liminoid" represents, in a sense, the dismembering, the *sparagmos* of the liminal; for various things that "hang together" in liminal situations split off to pursue separate destinies as specialized arts, and sports, and so on, as liminoid genres.[9]

In contrast to liminal states, liminoid ones do not develop within the core of society's traditions but on the fringes of the central structure of the society. For Turner, in literate cultures the "most articulate, conscious voices of values are the 'liminoid' poets, philosophers, dramatists, novelists, painters, and the like."[10] They show us our cultural building blocks, and we learn through their forages into the creative process. Turner regards metaphor as a "species of liminal monster . . . whose combination of familiar and unfamiliar features or unfamiliar combination of familiar features provokes us into thought and provides us with new perspectives."[11]

Such is the role of *Endgame*. Although Beckett uses few direct metaphors, the play itself functions as a metaphor; using basic objects (ladder, window, telescope, trashbin, whistle, handkerchief, clock), basic actions (sitting, standing, speaking), and basic processes (human interaction, growth, articulation, creation, change), the play imbues all of these with strangeness by their placement—or misplacement. Clov, who can only stand, is juxtaposed to Hamm, who can only sit. Standing and sitting become focal points which take on strangeness by such unusual attention. A painting faces the wall, garbage cans contain people, and nothing seems to change while all the while something takes its course. By the twist in usage, Beckett causes these simple things to resonate.

Words and their meanings have also been broken apart and set out of sync. Grammatical building blocks are exposed, showing that words are able to contradict and subvert each other by different combinations. According to Turner, "Syntax and logic are problematic and not axiomatic features of liminality."[12] Clov utters the first line of the play: "Finished, it's finished, nearly finished, it must be nearly finished." The play begins with the word, "finished," a paradox calling attention to our notions of beginning and ending. Hamm proclaims, "The end is in the beginning and yet you go on" (p. 69). The end is here literally in the beginning, pronounced with sureness, "Finished," and as the sentence begins its grammatical buildup, "Finished, it's finished, nearly finished, it must be nearly finished," is infused with doubt and even has the tone of a plea. Certainty has progressed to the point of a plea for the very certainty which sets the sentence in motion. This beginning sentence mimics the rest of the play— the buildup of uncertainty, the dispersion of sureness, and the loss of clarity as more words and attempts at action are added until it becomes a plea for an end. So, too, does Beckett portray life, and so, too, does he portray an artistic process which has become a tool to sustain and propel life.

The creative act can itself be a metaphor for the process of forming, with its various counterparts in life, death, and biological creation. However, unlike biology, artistic process is a very self-conscious act, and self-consciousness is a crucial "building block" of current times, one that is linked to liminality. Turner believes liminality is a stage at which there is a confrontation between structureless activity and the subsequent structure which results. This clash "produces in men their highest pitch of self-consciousness."[13] Clov and Hamm are a parody of self-conscious watching of the unstructured activity and the waiting, hoping, for a structured result to occur. Clov asks, "Why this farce day after day?" and Hamm replies, "Routine. One never knows" (p. 32). But something is taking its course, nonetheless, and change does occur—in their self-consciousness.

The idea of an end is a human conception imposed upon a mutating world, a root concept of human knowledge and culture, jockeyed by Beckett into the strange setting where it vibrates by its displacement, calling attention to itself and questioning its meaning. An end is a noun used to isolate a point where something changes, stops being one thing and starts being something we conceive of as different. It is a similar concept to that of the word, "edge," where a noun is used to designate a transition—the edge or end of a table stops; space begins. It is a point of change solidified into a noun concept. In discussing edges, Roland Barthes describes the "most erotic part of the body" as "*where the garment gapes . . . it is intermittence . . . between two edges . . . the staging of appearance-as-disappearance*."[14] It is as though Barthes takes the notion of the edge and turns it into a tunnel: the transition point or seam is enlarged to a space. He continues: "Two edges are created" when language is redistributed in a text, "an obedient, conformist, plagiarizing edge . . . and *another edge,* mobile, blank, (ready to assume any contours), which is never anything but the site of its effect: the place where the death of language is glimpsed."[15] The edge reveals itself as transition and glimmers with liminal peculiarities—the death of language is glimpsed here, and Hamm, in his last lines, proclaims, "Let's play it that way . . . and speak no more about it . . . speak no more" (p. 84).

The journey from speech to silence is a root paradigm of the play, closely aligned with the creative process. Turner notes that pilgrimage centers are usually on the periphery (as are the liminoid artists). To the believer, a pilgrimage center is a threshold or limen where he hopes to have immediate experience of the sacred or invisible which will be "efficacious in changing his inner and, sometimes, hopefully, outer conditions from sin to grace, or sickness to health."[16] Hamm takes a journey around the room and prays to God, only to conclude He does not exist and "there are no more sugar plums" (p. 55). The path from sin to grace, speech to silence, is blocked or nonexistent. Hamm has recourse only to the creative act of storytelling, or chronicle-making, for his salvation. One needs, then, to examine the author/character metaphor to see what kind of salvation, if any, the creative process provides, starting at the beginning of the play, in order to trace Clov's development as a character of Hamm's making and the result of this development upon Hamm.

The second line of the play describes accumulation: "Grain upon grain, one by one, and one day, suddenly, there's a heap, a little heap, the impossible heap" (p. 1). It is uttered by Clov, who presumably uses the words that Hamm has taught him. This idea is further developed and articulated by Hamm near the end of the play, after he has accumulated the experience portrayed within the play, and just before he learns there is no more painkiller: "Moment by moment, pattering down like the millet grains of . . .(He hesitates) . . . that Old Greek, and all life long you wait for that to mount up to a life" (p. 70). Clov, at the beginning of the play as an unfinished (or nearly finished) character, speaks in an abstract, unemotional manner; Hamm, at the end injects the idea with human experience—the craft of the author.

Hamm is the creator figure. He is seated kinglike center stage. He controls Clov's food, source of sustenance, and Clov in turn controls the painkiller; author nourishes character, and creative process eases, or at least distracts from, pain. Hamm is living, and Clov is a tool forged by him, a creative concoction and repository for Hamm's own experience. Clov, as character, is a means by which Hamm can deposit himself in something external. As author gives form to character, implanting seeds of his own thoughts, he raises him with the aim of making him real enough to stand on his own. Should Clov reach this goal, he would give Hamm a powerful glimpse into Hamm's own mind and heart and function as a landmark or blaze in his process of self-knowledge, a way to map out unknown territory.

Clov is nearly full-grown when the play begins; we enter after the groundwork has been laid and the end of the process begins to be felt: "Enough, it's time it ended, in the shelter too," Hamm declares after waking up. It is Hamm who first articulates the idea of Clov's leaving, and Clov picks it up and uses the thought much as a child learning a new word. In the beginning Clov gives only mirror-responses to Hamm which tell him nothing new; he matches words in kind but does not initiate or add:

HAMM: Why do you stay with me?
CLOV: Why do you keep me?

HAMM:	There's no one else.
CLOV	There's nowhere else. *(Pause.)*
HAMM:	You're leaving me all the same.
CLOV:	I'm trying.

(P. 6)

The idea of Clov's leaving builds throughout the play. The play begins with their mutual dependency and the struggle to separate mounts, gradually gaining momentum as Clov slowly learns:

HAMM:	Well! I thought you were leaving me.
CLOV:	Oh not just yet, not just yet.

(P. 9)

Hamm inquires about Clov's seeds, asking if they had come up yet, for, if they have, Clov will have gained his own independent source of nourishment:

CLOV:	They haven't sprouted.
HAMM:	Perhaps it's still too early.
CLOV:	If they were going to sprout they would have sprouted. *(Violently.)* They'll never sprout! . . .
HAMM:	This is not much fun.
		(Pause.) But that's always the way at the end of the day, isn't it, Clov? . . .
CLOV:	Looks like it.
		(Pause.)
HAMM:	*(Anguished):* What's happening, what's happening?
CLOV:	Something is taking its course.

(P. 13)

Clov's reply shows his point of development; he senses something is happening but can say no more about it. The struggle to continue proceeds. Hamm replies:

HAMM:	All right, be off. *(He leans back in his chair, remains motionless. Clov does not move, heaves a great groaning sigh. Hamm sits up.)*
		I thought I told you to be off.
CLOV:	I'm trying. *(He goes to door, halts.)*
		Ever since I was whelped. *(Exit Clov.)*
HAMM:	We're getting on.

(P. 14)

Clov obeys Hamm, much as a liminary obeys authority, and as a character must obey his creator. But controlling and guiding a character is difficult, slow work. When Hamm has Clov move him around the room, he quibbles and bickers about the slight inaccuracy of his position; he is not quite where he wants to be: Clov has moved him a "little too far to the left" and then a "little too far to the right" (p. 27). The purpose of the creative quest is to show him where it is he belongs, and his character is not yet able to do so satisfactorily. When Clov moves behind his chair, Hamm declares, "Don't stay there, you give me the shivers" (p. 27). Characters must remain in sight.

Clov's first purposeful act, and a sign of independence, comes when he climbs the ladder and drops the telescope, saying, "I did it on purpose" (p. 29). He picks it back up and turns it upon the audience: "I see . . . a multitude . . . in transports . . . of joy . . . That's what I call a magnifier" (p. 29). Clov is beginning to act on his own and develop a type of consciousness. A few lines later Hamm interrupts Clov when he begins to finish one of Hamm's own sentences and reprimands him with, "Wait till you're spoken to!" (p. 29). Although Hamm needs Clov's independence, he is threatened by its actual occurrence; Clov is his possession, under his control, and the knowledge that he is losing that control is unsettling. But lose it he must if he is to give life to his character.

The third time leaving is mentioned, it is Clov who initiates the discussion:

CLOV: So you all want me to leave you.
HAMM: Naturally.
CLOV: Then I'll leave you.
HAMM: You can't leave us.
CLOV: Then I won't leave you. *(Pause.)*
HAMM: Why don't you finish us? *(Pause.)*
I'll tell you the combination of the cupboard if you promise to finish me.
CLOV: I couldn't finish you.
HAMM: Then you won't finish me. *(Pause.)*
CLOV: I'll leave you, I have things to do.

(P. 37)

Clov has mentioned leaving more times than Hamm now. He states he will leave but cannot follow through, lapsing back into the stage where his dialogue merely matches Hamm ("You can't leave us—Then I won't leave you"). But Hamm yearns to be finished.

When Clov next declares, "I'll leave you" (p. 38), Hamm asks, "Did you never think of one thing?" Clov replies, "Never." Hamm continues his thought with, "We're down in a hole," meaning: Had it never occurred to Clov that they were down in a hole? Clov's inserted reply is humorously placed and creates the notion that, no, Clov is not able to think. Clov begins to think for himself as he begins to question his obedience:

CLOV: Do this, do that, and I do it, I never refuse. Why?
HAMM: You're not able to.
CLOV: Soon I won't do it any more.
HAMM: You won't be able to any more.

(P. 43)

A reversal takes place when Hamm states, "I can't leave you," and Clov replies, "I know. And you can't follow me" (p. 45). Here Hamm acknowledges Clov's leaving, and by doing so acknowledges Clov's power: his creation is no longer his possession and Hamm will be forced to look upon his creative issue, that which has split off from him and come round to face him with his own image. Hamm asks, "If you leave me how shall I know?" (p. 45) and angrily urges Clov to "think of something," to "have an idea. A bright idea!" (p. 46). After painful pacing, Clov has an idea: in order to let Hamm know whether he has left or died, he will set the alarm clock; if it rings, he has left, and if it doesn't, he has died. He gives Hamm a sample ring, proclaiming, "Fit to wake the dead . . . The end is terrific!" (p. 48). To Clov the alarm signifies his completion and release; to Hamm it is the end of his involvement with this character. As the creative process is a painkiller for Hamm, Clov's departure means he will feel full-strength pain again. To ease the pain, he must either die or start again. Hamm "prefers the middle," and asks, "Is it not time for my pain-killer?" Clov responds, "No! I'll leave you" (p. 48).

After bribing his father to listen (perhaps a parody of the literary father), Hamm begins his monologue with lines similar to those which opened the play: "It's finished, we're finished. Nearly finished. There'll be no more speech" (p. 50). This time a *"we're* finished" has replaced the *"it's* finished" of the first line, and a glimpse of what is to come is added—no more speech; Clov's abstract sentence has become more fleshed out with human sense. The play is taking its course. Hamm recounts his story, fully worked out until the point where a decision must be made: "It was the moment I was waiting for. *(Pause.)* Would I consent to take in the child . . ." (p. 53). He ceases his narrative tone of voice and says:

I'll soon have finished with this story. *(Pause.)*
Unless I bring in other characters. *(Pause.)*
But where would I find them? *(Pause.)*
Where would I look for them? *(Pause. He whistles. Enter Clov.)* Let us pray to God.

(P. 54)

The epitome of the self-conscious writer, Hamm spins his world around himself; he is Beckett's character weaving the very play in which he exists, man without God. His story seems to be of the origin of Clov.

Physical manifestations of Clov's leaving begin. He realizes he has put
on his boots when Hamm calls attention to the different sound of his feet.
Hamm appeals to his story to retain him:

CLOV: I'll leave you.
HAMM: No!
CLOV: What is there to keep me here?
HAMM: The dialogue. *(Pause.)* I've got on with it well.
       (Pause. Irritably.) Ask me where I've got to.

(P. 58)

Next begins a series of promptings by Hamm to push Clov to sustain and
contribute to the dialogue; he pushes his character to speak back to him:

HAMM: Ask me where I've got to.
CLOV: Oh, by the way, your story?
HAMM: *(Surprised):* What story?
CLOV: The one you've been telling yourself all your days.
HAMM: Ah you mean my chronicle?
CLOV: That's the one. *(Pause.)*
HAMM: *(Angrily):* Keep going, can't you, keep going!

(P. 58)

The dialogue continues to spin its wheel, trying to get somewhere,
getting nowhere, and all the while getting on with it:

CLOV: You've got on with it, I hope.
HAMM: *(Modestly):* Oh not very far, not very far. *(He sighs.)* There are
       days like that, one isn't inspired. *(Pause.)* No forcing, no forc-
       ing, it's fatal. I've got on with it a little all the same.
CLOV: *(Admiringly):* Well I never! In spite of everything you were able
       to get on with it!
HAMM: *(Modestly):* Oh not very far, you know, not very far, but never-
       theless, better than nothing.
CLOV: Better than nothing! Is it possible?

(P. 59)

The dialogue sounds like a lot of talk about nothing—the imperceptible
moments of the struggle with nothing to come up with something that is
the play. As Hamm continues to tell Clov his story, Clov begins to add
parts about himself:

HAMM: I continue then. Before accepting with gratitude he asks if he
       may have his little boy with him.
CLOV: What age?
HAMM: Oh tiny.
CLOV: He would have climbed the trees.

HAMM: All the little odd jobs.
CLOV: And then he would have grown up.
HAMM: Very likely. *(Pause.)*
CLOV: Keep going, can't you, keep going!
HAMM: That's all. I stopped there. *(Pause.)*

(Pp. 60–61)

Hamm stops at the point of Clov's present development. Clov, as character, has enough self-consciousness to realize he has a future, a fate, and he wants to know what it is:

CLOV: Do you see how it goes on.
HAMM: More or less.
CLOV: Will it not soon be the end?
HAMM: I'm afraid it will.
CLOV: Pah! You'll make up another.
HAMM: I don't know. *(Pause.)* I feel rather drained. *(Pause.)* The prolonged creative effort.

(P. 61)

Just prior to Clov's leaving, Hamm anxiously contemplates the end: "Perhaps I could go on with my story, end it and begin another. *(Pause.)* Perhaps I could throw myself out on the floor" (p. 69). He pictures himself alone "against the silence and . . .*(He hesitates)* . . . The stillness" (p. 69). He aims at the peace of silence but it slides into an uneasy stillness; he has not reached salvation yet. He imagines having called to his father, and to his son, and received no answer. The aloneness—of stillness, not silence—sinks in:

HAMM: And then? *(Pause. Very agitated.)* All kinds of fantasies! That I'm being watched! A rat! Steps! Breath held and then . . . *(He breathes out.)* Then babble, babble, words, like the solitary child who turns himself into children, two, three, so as to be together, in the dark.

(P. 70)

The tension, fears, and fantasies, contained and held within are the crucible in which Hamm's anxieties are channeled into the survival means of creativity—the exhalation and projection of himself into something else, a compulsive, necessary means to ease his separateness. Hence the existence of Clov. With Clov gone, the "babble, babble" of words will roil and swell again. Peace can only come when the impetus is gone. At this point for Hamm, impetus remains.

The rat in the kitchen gets away, the painkiller runs out for Hamm, and Clov begins winding up the alarm clock, humming, and declares, "I want to sing" (p. 73). Hamm acknowledges his loss of power with, "I can't prevent you." Something has taken its course and is about to break, but there was no moment when something happened, no moment when the change occurred, but change it did. There is no moment when a character acquires full-bodiedness and life, or when a play or work of art gathers its own impetus, but it did. Hamm professes his despair of the end: "Absent, always. It all happened without me. I don't know what's happened" (p. 74).

When Clov spots a small boy out of the window, Hamm questions his existence. Clov replies, "You don't believe me? You think I'm inventing?" Hamm's response is certain: "It's the end, Clov, we've come to the end. I don't need you any more" (p. 79). For if Clov can think of inventing, he can invent, he has his own seeds of creativity. Having created another creator, Hamm's and Clov's mutual dependency dissolves; they are both separate now. Now it is time for Clov to give to Hamm. Hamm asks Clov, prompting him with dialogue, to say something from his "heart" (p. 80). Clov struggles, "*(despairingly)* Ah . . .!" He has had thoughts, an idea, an urge to sing, and a flash of creativity. He must now take his newly acquired substance and articulate it, not intellectually, but as a genuine extension of his being. What Clov gives Hamm in his speech is a summation of Hamm's own beliefs, manifested in his own words. Clov speaks of love, friendship, beauty, and the orderliness of clear thinking; this is how "they" had instructed him to think—concepts of harmony which are inadequate, sterile. They are the ones "dying of their wounds" (p. 80). Hamm cries, "Enough!" at this point, not fully ready to face his own creed for the first time. But Hamm has done his job well; Clov continues on his own impetus articulating to Hamm what Hamm has been struggling to say:

> CLOV: I say to myself—sometimes, Clov, you must learn to suffer better than that if you want them to weary of punishing you—one day. I say to myself—sometimes, Clov, you must be there better than that if you want them to let you go—one day. But I feel old, and too far, to form new habits. Good, it'll never end, I'll never go.
> (Pp. 80–81)

Clov has summed up the slow agony of the play, the waiting for some moment to come, "one day" which will change things. This paragraph of his speech is a sophisticated development of the rudimentary sentence he first uttered, beginning with "Finished." Hamm had said, "The end is in the beginning and yet you go on" (p. 69). For the end version above is a revision of the beginning sentence. It is now suffused with the profundity and experience of what has taken place in between during the play. The certainty Clov expresses here is that it will never be finished. Paradoxically, at the point where Clov admits defeat in his speech, things change:

> CLOV: *(Pause.)* Then one day, suddenly, it ends, it changes. I don't understand, it dies, or it's me. I don't understand, that either. I

ask the words that remain—sleeping, waking, morning, evening.
They have nothing to say.

(P. 81)

Clov describes the change without understanding it; this paragraph
mirrors the sudden change of the second line in the play: "Grain upon
grain, one by one, and one day, suddenly, there's a heap, a little heap, the
impossible heap." The change is no longer about "the impossible heap"
but is instead the dissolution of it, a change to the realm beyond the power
of words, where the death of language is glimpsed. Words of beginnings
and endings, "sleeping, waking, morning, evening," are no longer charged
with meaning. Released from such concepts, Clov is free:

CLOV: I open the door of the cell and go. I am so bowed I only see my
feet, if I open my eyes, and between my legs a little trail of black
dust. I say to myself that the earth is extinquished, though I never
saw it lit. *(Pause.)*
It's easy going. When I fall I'll weep for happiness.

(P. 81)

Clov has articulated the central message of Hamm's life. Hamm comes
face to face with himself through Clov and sees the direction of his own
life. It is a tragic paradox of freedom and brokenness. Clov exits and
comes back, dressed for the road, but does not make his presence known
to Hamm. He stands facing him. As a character he will always face his
creator; he now has a life of his own, unseen, unknown to his creator, but
is nonetheless always pointing back to his origin.

Hamm makes ready for his closing monologue. He gives a little poetry:
"You cried for night; it falls: now cry in darkness" (p. 83). His crying has
not stopped; he is not complete, he is without salvation. This act of
creativity is over: "Moments for nothing, now as always, time was never
and time is over, reckoning closed and story ended" (p. 83). He picks up
his story where he had left it:

If he could have his child with him . . . *(Pause.)* It was the moment I was
waiting for. *(Pause.)* You don't want to abandon him? You want him to
bloom while you are withering? Be there to solace your last million last
moments? *(Pause.)* He doesn't realize, all he knows is hunger, cold, and
death to crown it all. But you! You ought to know what the earth is like,
nowadays. O I put him before his responsibilities!

(P. 83)

The end of Hamm's story sums up what Clov has shown him. He has
produced a character embodying the tragedy of life, recounted in Clov's
ending speech. His admonishment to the crawling man wanting to have his
child shows the immense weight and responsibility of producing such an

embodiment of misery. In his story Hamm gives the man no definite answer, but leaves him before the enormity of his responsibilities—that is what he has learned from Clov. Artistic process is no light matter.

Through the creative act, Hamm has given form to the building blocks of his existence: the will to push for completion, and the knowledge that each necessary step toward completion is full of responsibility. Hamm cannot remain stagnant in time, and, as a liminoid creator no longer inscribed within a set ritual governed by authority, he must take total responsibility for his own transformation. By exhausting his creative impetus, he seeks to build his salvation. He has no assurance salvation awaits his strenuous efforts, but he nonetheless pushes for an exhaustive silence which will bring him peace.

Hamm proceeds to discard his dog and throws his whistle—instrument of control—to the audience, "With my compliments" (p. 84). His work of art is completed, and so too is another step toward an imagined salvation. He declares he will "speak no more about it" as he unfolds his handkerchief, that which has caught his blood, recording the suffering of a life: "Old stancher! You . . . remain" (p. 84). Thus remains the play, catcher of blood and suffering, recorder of transition and growth.

Notes

1. Samuel Beckett, *Endgame* (New York: Grove Press, 1958), p. 13. Subsequent quotations are from this edition.

2. David Hesla, *The Shape of Chaos* (Minneapolis: University of Minnesota Press, 1971), p. 153. Hannah Case Copeland also discusses Beckett's obsession with the creative act in *Art and the Artist in the Works of Samuel Beckett* (The Hague, Netherlands: Mouton, 1975), exploring his quest for the self through creation. Sidney Homan pursues a similar theme with Hamm as playwright and Clov as actor in *"Endgame:* The Playwright Completes Himself" in *Beckett's Theatre: Interpretations for Performance* (London & Toronto: Bucknell University Press, 1984), pp. 58–78.

3. Victor Turner, *Dramas, Fields, and Metaphors* (Ithaca, N. Y.: Cornell University Press, 1974), p. 51.

4. Victor Turner, "Variations on a Theme of Liminality," *Secular Ritual,* eds. Sally F. Moore and Barbara G. Myerhoff (Assen, The Netherlands: Van Gorcum, 1977), p. 37.

5. Victor Turner, *The Ritual Process* (Chicago: Aldine, 1969), p. 15.

6. Turner, *Dramas,* p. 297.

7. Ibid., p. 50.

8. Beckett, as quoted in Ann Cremin, "Friendgame," *Artnews* (May 1985): 87.

9. Turner, "Variations," p. 43.

10. Turner, *Dramas,* p. 17.

11. Ibid., p. 31.

12. Ibid., p. 255.

13. Ibid.

14. Roland Barthes, *The Pleasure of the Text,* trans. Richard Miller (New York: Hill and Wang, 1975), p. 9.

15. Ibid., p. 6.

16. Turner, *Dramas,* p. 197.

MYTH AND DEMYTHIFICATION

Beckett by Way of Baudrillard

Toward a Political Reading of Samuel Beckett's Drama

Stephen Watt

VLADIMIR: "Hand in hand from the top of the Eiffel Tower, among the first. We were respectable in those days."[1]

ESTRAGON: "That's where we'll go, I used to say, that's where we'll go for our honeymoon. We'll swim. We'll be happy."

(P. 8r)

1. Ritual and "Green-World" Myth in Beckett's Plays

Nearly all of the problems of this brief meditation on Samuel Beckett's drama—and one problematic central to this drama—are registered in the title of my opening section: "Ritual and 'Green-World' Myth in Beckett's Plays." What "ritual"? What "myth"? What "green world"? If these questions were not enough with which to contend, one might also wonder how such questions relate to a political reading of Beckett's drama. More fundamental questions arise in the notion of a "political" reading of Beckett. With few exceptions, most Marxist critics have echoed Georg Lukács's disdain for the ahistorical, allegorical, bourgeois work of Beckett, Kafka, and others.[2] It's time this position was reassessed. In this introduction, I should like to privilege both "ritual" and "green-world" myth as figures of a problematic in Beckett's drama that is crucial to any preliminary interrogation of its political or social dimensions. As I define these, I shall also deploy (provisionally) "ritual" and "myth" as binary opposites: hence, ritual/myth or—given their trajectories in Beckett's plays—social structuration/"green-world" antistructure. An often abused term, "problematic" is used here as an explanatory tool in precisely the way John Fekete conceives of it: a "social, ideological, or theoretical framework within which complexes of problems are structured and single problems acquire density, meaning and significance."[3] It is my contention that Beckett's plays—while perhaps lacking in the typicality, concrete social context, and totality that Lukács values in "realism"—are nevertheless shaped squarely within a discouragingly familiar bourgeois horizon

103

and its dominant symbolic and institutional formations, formations unmasked by inquiry into this problematic. Moreover, a number of single
problems—the commodification of objects, the controlling ideology attached to them, and their signification in exchange—might all be revalued
within the poles of this theoretical framework. Crucial to this revaluation
is the work of Jean Baudrillard, to whom I shall turn repeatedly while
describing a powerful, ultimately determining formation which is "always
and already there" in Samuel Beckett's drama.

The questions posed above—ones concerning ritual, myth, and green
world—might be addressed by reference to one passage from Beckett's
early story "The Expelled" (1946). Cited by Hugh Kenner some years ago
as an instance of Beckett's characters contriving to "kill time" by "re-
hearsing their grasp of detail,"[4] the passage is even more revelatory of a
problematic central to his plays:

> Even as I fell I heard the door slam, which brought me a little comfort,
> in the midst of my fall. For that meant they were not pursuing me down
> into the street. . . . If that had been their intention they would not have
> closed the door, but left it open, so that the persons assembled in the
> vestibule might enjoy my chastisement and be edified. So, for once, they
> had confined themselves to throwing me out. . . . I rested my elbow on
> the sidewalk. . . . But the sound, fainter but unmistakable, of the door
> slammed again, roused me from my reverie, where already a whole
> landscape was taking form, charming with hawthorn and wild roses,
> most dreamlike. (P. 194)

This scene bears structural affinity with numerous "fallings" or separa-
tions in Beckett's plays. Expelled from his home and its defined social
status (child-son), the narrator finds himself for once lying statusless on
the pavement. A series of public chastisements and pursuits have
seemingly stripped him of his former status; mercifully, the first slamming
of the door concludes what had become a ritualized violence. And, like
many of Beckett's characters, the narrator must actively seek or passively
await the social reintegration to which such rituals usually lead. I employ
"ritual" here in its most secular sense to describe moments in Beckett's
plays in which repetitive, formalized actions bear close relationship to the
attaining or reconfirming of social status or institutional standing. However, for Beckett's characters new status is never easily attained. Like
others, the narrator of "The Expelled" must undergo a transitional period,
one which Arnold van Gennep and Victor Turner after him call "liminality": the state of being "betwixt and between the categories of ordinary social life."[5]

In Beckett's plays, the liminal figure's lack of clearly defined status need
not inhibit imagination or obliterate memory. For these characters—un-

like, say, Mercier and Camier in Beckett's fiction, who are able to travel to the country yet cannot sever their ties to the city—memory and dreams constitute the only vehicle for transcending social organization or escaping categorization. In "The Expelled" the dream of hawthorns and wild roses offers momentary relief from the sidewalk, just as Nell's recollections of Lake Como in *Endgame* counter the stench of her dustbin and Winnie's memories of the back garden at Borough Green in *Happy Days* irrigate momentarily her scorched burial mound. But are such evocations of natural beauty or the "green world" in Beckett's plays motivated solely by the extreme conditions of characters like Winnie and Nell? Are such evocations, coupled as they usually are with nostalgic reminiscence, indicative of what S. E. Gontarski has recently termed "a longing for some form of stability, if not an ideal core at least a core of some sort, a center"?[6] What relationship obtains between this vegetable world and social status? And do brief dreams like the narrator's exert only a temporary effect?

Probably not, as Northrop Frye's discussion of the mythos of spring and the "green world" suggests. For Frye, the term "green world" not only delimits a place of natural beauty and social transformation, but also describes a comic narrative of social consequence. The narrative movement in green-world drama is familiar to most of us: as Frye describes it, this drama replicates the "ritual theme of the triumph of life and love over the wasteland."[7] Such triumphs are accomplished in Shakespeare's *The Two Gentlemen of Verona, A Midsummer Night's Dream,* and *As You Like It* in part because of the transforming journeys to forests and enchanted woods which Shakespeare's central characters so routinely take. (Note that the journeys of characters in Beckett's fiction—Watt, Mercier, and Camier for instance—seldom end in any transformation or social integration.) As Duke Senior in *As You Like It* describes the Forest of Arden, the luxuriant green world, inhabited by "brothers in exile," is more "free of peril than the envious court" and immune to the "seasons' differences" and the "penalty of Adam."[8] Hence, the green world is immune to the very predicaments of Beckett's characters and ourselves caused by Adam's fall: the implicit fragmentation of the Edenic totality. Allusions to natural beauty in Beckett's plays are both resonant of the qualities of Frye's "green world" and, further, steeped in a utopian myth of coherence in which Beckett's characters occasionally find great consolation. Nevertheless, such allusions also constitute an ultimately self-deluding fiction of transcendence. Moreover, such moments in Beckett's drama are often saturated with the very institutional or social values which undermine the green world's "purity" or essential status.

More important, however, the green world in Beckett's plays forms a mythic space which opposes ritual and the social structure which en-

dorses it. Here I turn again to van Gennep and Victor Turner. Van Gennep
maintains that rites of passage are comprised of three smaller formal units:
rites of separation, transition, and incorporation. (Here it is important to
explain that "incorporation" does not denote a totalizing integration, a
realization of Freud's "oceanic" feeling, but an assimilation into a social
class or category.) Rites of separation, ones which are seldom completed
for Beckett's characters, crucially eradicate the initiate's former (preliminal) social position by stripping him of all "signs or insignias" of this
status (*DFM*, p. 53). The initiand, in transition between the social formation from which he or she has been cleaved and a new social formation
into which he or she will eventually be incorporated, exists outside or on
the periphery of the conditions and constraints of social organization.
Consequently, Turner observes, as the liminal character is released from
the legislation of any social formation, he enters a condition of *communitas*—an "antistructure" in which a "bond" uniting initiates (presuming
there is more than one) exists "over and above any formal social bonds"
(*DFM*, p. 53). In the green world of, say, *As You Like It, communitas*
signifies a brotherhood "in exile" and an opposition to the "envious
court." *Communitas*, then, stands in opposition to hierarchy or structure;
if the purpose of structure is to define social differences and keep people
apart, the green world and *communitas* imply the possibility of a structureless union.

Of course, the Beckettian design never admits *communitas* or incorporation; on the contrary, it seems to foreground unsuccessful rites of
separation (Clov, W in *Rockaby,* the Speaker in *A Piece of Monologue*) or
transition (Didi and Gogo, Winnie). In the passage from "The Expelled"
above, Beckett inscribes several possible causes for this dilemma, the
most potent of which originates in the initiate's incomplete separation
from the social formation he is leaving (or being forced to leave). In "The
Expelled" the narrator recalls gazing up in alarm as the sound of a second
door slam awakens him from the reverie "charming with hawthorn and
wild roses":

> It was merely my hat sailing towards me through the air, rotating as it
> came. I caught it and put it on. . . . The spell was broken. (Pp. 194–95)

The narrator's hat, as he almost consciously acknowledges, functions as a
sign of his preliminal status as child-son. Next, the narrator recalls his
father taking him to buy it, revealing the powerful hierarchy the hat
represents:

> Come, son, we are going to buy your hat, as though it had pre-existed
> from time immemorial in a pre-established place. . . . It was forbidden
> me, from that day forth, to go out bareheaded. (P. 195)

The hat signifies, among other things, the narrator's position as son. His submission to his father's legislation about wearing it intimates that he, like so many of Beckett's characters, has not yet effected a clear division from a former personal and social formation. Even though in the past the hat provided the occasion for the narrator's derision by boys in his neighborhood and even though after his father's death the narrator might violate his father's injunction, he defers to "some other time, some other time" an explanation of why as an adult he continues to wear it. As he walks clumsily away from the home he had so seldom left before, with the sign of his preliminal status perched on his head, the narrator detects in a policeman's order an insinuation that he "could not be assimilated into the category of everyone else." Thus, the hat—which has shattered the dream of a "green world" and its "spell" of "charming" nature—accompanies the narrator to wreak its determining mischief as he seeks a new social category and an "assimilation" for which the "green world" serves as metaphor.

The relationship between these two fairly typical phenomena in Beckett's plays—signs of a past social standing and dreams of a "green-world" transcendence—might also be rearticulated in other ways. On the one hand, for example, Vivian Mercier regards allusions to natural beauty in *Happy Days, How It is,* and *Play* as evidence of a character's former status as "upper middle class."[9] In this reading, the green world serves merely as a metonymic figure of past affluence and class affiliation and is thus congruent with, not opposed to, society and social ritual. On the other hand, as the passage in "The Expelled" concerning the narrator's hat and his pastoral reverie indicates, the relationship between social status and nature in Beckett often appears to be oppositional. Recall the hat and its signifying functions: when the green world as a figure of transcendence rises to apparent ascendancy, it is destroyed by the hat and the ideology attached to it. In this context, the green world symbolizes selfhood, escape from social responsibility or regimentation. Hence, perhaps Beckett's green world approaches that of feminists such as Annis Pratt, who have speculated that in much modern fiction the "advent of selfhood" and "sensual blossoming of the psyche" are "heralded" by an "epiphanic vision of the green world."[10] Would this not be an apt description of the reverie of hawthorn and wild roses—an "epiphanic vision of the green world"? And while the narrator's "sensual blossoming" is not indicated in "The Expelled," numerous characters in Beckett (male and female) express past sexual awakenings through imagery of natural beauty. Winnie in *Happy Days* remembers the back garden at Borough Green under the horse-beech and immediately recalls Charlie Hunter and her first kiss; in his tape, Krapp glowingly recounts placing his face in a woman's breasts while moving gently on a lake on a sunny afternoon. And even though he later repudiates his own stupidity, he nevertheless concedes he could have been "happy with her, up there on the Baltic, and the pines, and the dunes" (p. 25). From this perspective, the Beckettian green world is a memorial to sexuality and a location of escape. It is, finally, a myth, perhaps, as Simone de Beauvoir posits, a patriarchal one: "For the young girl, for the woman who has not fully abdicated, nature represents what woman herself represents for man: herself and her negation, a kingdom and a place of exile."[11] In a paradigm derived from this view, the binarism ritual/green-world may be adequated to others like society/ selfhood, culture/ nature, thereby representing more than only sexual awakening. Sadly, both impulses—one pulling toward the green world, the other toward society—are most often equivalent, with the latter impulse generally exhibiting superior strength. Herein lies the problematic of many a Beckett play, though characters in various texts respond to its pressures in very different ways.

Consider the cases of Vladimir and Estragon. As Vivian Mercier emphasizes, Beckett's two tramps appeared more "shabby-genteel" than "ragged" in the first Paris staging of *Waiting for Godot,* carrying with them sartorial, linguistic, and other clues of their past social position.[12] Vladimir nostalgically recalls being "among the first" at the top of the Eiffel Tower in "those days" when he and Estragon were "respectable." Their "shabby gentility"—much like Winnie's dress and pearls, Willie's tuxedo, and W's "black lacy high-necked evening gown" in *Rockaby*— signals their preliminal bourgeois status. However, Estragon, who complains later in *Godot* that he either forgets the past "immediately" or never forgets it, counters Vladimir's reminiscence of past respectability with an indelibly etched memory of the map of the Dead Sea:

> That's where we'll go I used to say, that's where we'll go for our honeymoon. We'll swim. We'll be happy. (P. 8r)

Like Nell's memories of Lake Como, Estragon's nostalgic recollection (factual or not) celebrates the idealized equality, secure selfhood, and heightened sensuality of the green world. Here, in little more than a minute, Didi and Gogo evoke images of two opposing modes of social organization: the hierarchical Parisian society and a classless site of union far distanced from the Champs-Elysées. In this context allusions to the green world serve not to reinforce the privilege of "respectability" or social class, but to underscore the inadequacy of "respectability" in satisfying human needs. While the irony of celebrating a honeymoon in a body of water named "dead" intimates the self-deluding nature of Estragon's project, his memory at least provides a counterpoise to Vladimir's and to the notion that Beckett's characters suffer most because of their loss of elevated social status.

In fact this opposition—the desire to acquire, regain, or maintain a defined location in a social hierarchy and the opposing impulse, symbolized by the green world, to escape from such a hierarchy—emerges in *Godot, Endgame, Happy Days,* and others. The strength of the former impulse in these plays is considerable indeed. For example, Vladimir recommends to Estragon that before hanging themselves they ought to "know exactly" how they "stand" with Godot ((p. 12r); after all, so long as "one knows what to expect," one can "bide one's time" (p. 25r). In *Endgame,* Hamm's insistence that he be placed "right in the center" (p. 26), "bang in the center" (p. 27) after his turn "right round the world" (p. 25) reveals a similar desire for a secure niche in the social world. Still, like Krapp, Winnie, and the characters Pratt examines, Hamm associates the green world with both escape and sexual awakening:

> If I could sleep I might make love. I'd go into the woods. My eyes would see . . . the sky, the earth. I'd run, they wouldn't catch me. (P. 18)

Just as quickly, and this attests to the power of social structuration, Hamm dismisses the possibility that "the earth will awake in spring," that the "rivers and seas will run with fish again" (p. 53). Consequently, he contrives rituals which serve only to preserve the status quo of his kingdom. Not surprisingly, it is his recognition that time and nature do exist—"But we breathe, we change! We lose our hair, our teeth! Our bloom! Our ideals!" (p. 11)—that leads to his elaboration of rituals to resist such changes. Disturbances such as the flea, the rat, and especially the boy Clov reports seeing later in *Endgame* reveal the conservative functioning of its rituals, one René Girard sees as the sole purpose of all ritual:

> The sole purpose of ritual is to ensure total immobility, or failing that, a minimum of disturbances. If the door is opened to admit change, there is always the risk that violence or chaos will force an entry.[13]

For Girard, such rituals center around the scapegoat, that "exemplary guarantor of cultural stability" against whom "unanimous violence is directed."[14] The narrator of "The Expelled," Estragon, fleas in *Endgame,* and young rodents in *Watt* might all qualify for this unenviable part as scapegoats in Beckett.

Clov, whose primary objective is to effect a lasting separation from Hamm's tyranny, represents the opposite impulse in *Endgame*—to grasp for the "life to come," not to conserve the life that is. As we know, Clov has been and may continue to be ineffectual in achieving such a separation—the problem that with an even more excruciating pain plagues the central characters of Beckett's most recent plays. And perhaps the collision between the desire for secure social categorization and the opposing

desire to elude such structuring partially accounts for Clov's failure.
Ironically, while at the beginning of *Endgame* Hamm awakens reporting
dreams of forests ("What forests!")—dreams he quickly dismisses and
ritualistically abolishes—Clov harbors desires for the very ordering from
which he would free himself:

> I love order. It's my dream. A world where all would be silent and still
> and each thing in its place, under the last dust. (P. 57).

My point here is that neither Hamm nor Clov can successfully suppress
his opposing desires—for structural differentiation in Clov's case and the
antistructure of the green world in Hamm's. Consequently, their rituals are
both undone by their "dreams," dreams which parasitically devour their
hosts, the ritualistic attempts to neutralize the power of opposing impulses.[15]

This deconstructive undermining of seemingly stable oppositions continues to dominate more recent theatrical pieces such as *A Piece of
Monologue* and *Rockaby*. In *A Piece of Monologue,* the speaker informs
us of his daily or nightly routine: he arises "every nightfall," "gropes to
window and stares out," strikes matches in a particular order, and so on.
His last words—"Alone gone"—ostensibly refer to the light dying in the
globe he has lit earlier. The narrator, too, is in the most literal sense alone
and contemplating the day of "being gone." But so long as he is "being,"
there is no such thing as "gone." As he reminds us, there is "no such thing
as whole" (p. 14), yet there is "no such thing as none" either (p. 12). His
pictures of the "loved ones," the phrase he "all but says" and then does
say, are not all gone—some pins are "still pinning a shred" of pictures on
his wall (p. 12). The picture of his parent's wedding day and the evocation
of familial affection rush through his mind, internally opposing the
nothingness of the present and obstructing his endeavor to "Move on to
other matters. Try to move on. To other matters" (p. 14). Perhaps "W" in
Rockaby comes closer to demolishing this opposition. Both the narrative
progression of the recorded voice and the final halting of her rocking at the
play's end intimate that she may have accomplished what Girard sees as
the end of all ritual—complete immobility. The narrative progress of her
recording leads to such immobility: from the time she stopped "*going*
(emphasis mine) to and fro" for "another like herself" (pp. 19, 20, 21), to
the time she stopped "*sitting*" (emphasis mine) and looking for another
(p. 23), to the time she emulated her mother, who put on her "best black"
and rocked "till her end came" (p. 24). The rocking—a conservative ritual
intended as a safeguard against change or the hope for change—is coun-
tered by the listening which it is time she stopped but has not. The
collision between ritual and myth continues in the Beckettian abyss,

signaling both the strength of ideology and failure of society to satisfy human needs.

2. The "Always Already There" in Beckett's Drama

As I suggested above, the ritual/myth binarism is a provisional structure which finally must be dismantled, simply because it conceals the power of bourgeois ideology in Beckett. But to effect this dismantling and subsequent unveiling, one must not be persuaded by several more or less "typical" surface features of Beckett's drama that it is somehow devoid of all historical meaning. One such feature, for instance, is the apparent distance between the theatrical space (temporal and geographic) of Beckett's drama and any recognizable sociohistorical context.[16] Lukács sees in this dislocation of time from historical change and particularity of place the vestiges of subjective Idealism, a rupture between text and world. In Lukács's terms, because these plays are situated beyond social boundaries (or possibly after society's destruction in some cases), the "dialectical unity between inner and outer worlds is destroyed, and both individual and society consequently emptied of meaning."[17] However, if this were indeed the case, if no social forces exerted any determining influence, then of course there would be no hint of rites of separation or transition in Beckett's drama. As I have tried to demonstrate above—and as Katherine Burkman and Susan Brienza, among others, have argued—Beckett's plays are constituted of several ritual patterns.[18] But more than ritual is involved here. The finally untranscendable horizons of social and economic formations in, say, *Happy Days, Endgame,* and *Waiting for Godot* are analogous to Michel Foucault's systems of symbolic, discursive, and institutional power: they are "always already there," operating in objects like the narrator's hat in "The Expelled."

If this hat does serve as a figure of determining power in Beckett, then its presence might invite a larger inquiry into Beckettian objects and their relationship to his characters. And an inquiry of this kind can only be aided by Jean Baudrillard's ruminations about consumption and commodification, which serve to correct any privileging or mystification of the *use value* of objects over their *exchange value.* That is, the emphasis of use value appears almost as a given in most Beckett studies, precisely because of the dismal material conditions of his characters. The appeals to this materiality are by now quite familiar. Surely in these desperate conditions objects are consumed or services rendered on the basis of need; the economy of most Beckett plays is, after all, marked by scarcity. But will this "natural, anthropological" interpretation of need and its implicit evaluation of objects on the criterion of utility adequately explain the overdetermined value and operation of the narrator's hat in "The Expelled"?

More broadly, will it illuminate the functions of other objects in Beckett's work? Hardly. What seems necessary here is, as Baudrillard might put it, shattering of an antiquated mirror of production which has distorted (or occluded) the logic of consumption:

> An analysis of the social logic which regulates the practice *(pratique)* of objects according to diverse classes or categories cannot help but be at the same time a critical analysis of the ideology of "consumption". . . . This double analysis—that of the distinctive social function of objects and of the political function of the ideology that is attached to it—must be based upon . . . the surpassing of a spontaneous vision of objects in terms of needs and the hypothesis of the priority of their use value.[19]

Instead, Baudrillard maintains, an object's "sign exchange value" *(valeur d'échange signe)* is fundamental, use value being little more than a practical guarantee of (or even a rationalization pure and simple for) consumption. Consumption, as Baudrillard rather boldly postulates, has "nothing to do with personal enjoyment": rather, it is a "restrictive social institution that determines behavior before ever being considered in the consciousness of the social actor" *(PE,* p. 31). Like the narrator in "The Expelled" who quite automatically catches the hat, puts it on, and then defers giving any explanation of his actions, many Beckett characters behave in manners determined by objects and a potent logic of consumption which both operates them and generates "need."

Baudrillard's critique of consumption rests upon his homologous structuring of exchange value/use value and signifier/signified, an articulation in which ideology plays a crucial, formative role. For Baudrillard, ideology, "whose allegorical power somehow insinuates itself into consciousnesses . . . in order to integrate them," lies *"already whole in the relation of EV* [Exchange Value] *to UV* [Use Value], *that is, in the logic of the commodity,* as is so in the relation of Sr [Signifier] to Sd [Signified], i.e. in the internal logic of the sign" (Baudrillard's emphasis; *PE,* p. 144). In less tortuous prose, in the "logic of the commodity" use value serves at best as a satellite (an ancillary role), at worst as an alibi for a larger system that determines exchange and encodes it with social meanings. Hence, an object's use value disguises its operation as a commodity, its signifying function in a system of exchange. Similarly, the signified-referent amounts merely to a "mirage," the absolute separability of the sign and the world a fiction: the "world" (reality) that the sign evokes is "nothing but the effect of the sign."

This "logic" manifests itself time and time again in Beckett's plays, revealing its ideological genesis in class-consciousness, prestige, the family, and other all-too-familiar values and institutions. One political or social critique *within* a Beckett play, then, is located in the ideological value attached to the commodification and encoding of objects (including costumes and properties) in *Happy Days, Waiting for Godot, Endgame,* and others. These same values, not nature, God, or other origins of the characters' predicaments in existential explanations, also form an absolute horizon which the Beckettian subject cannot transcend. From this perspective, the ritual/myth binarism which I posited above as a provisional framework for reading Beckett's drama might now be dismantled, or perhaps regarded as homologous to EV/UV and Sr/Sd. That is, the "green-world" myth acts as "alibi" for the dominance of ritual, social categorization, and hegemonic power; *communitas,* Turner's "antistructure" of bonds existing "over and above any formal social bonds" between men and men (and men and nature), becomes as fictional as use value or the signified. In short, there are no bonds in Beckett's work purely "outside" of society's regulation.

This may seem to be an especially radical claim about Beckett's plays. By contrast, the domination of characters by objects and the social values attached to them would seem much more compelling in novels like *Mercier and Camier.* As the narrator explains toward the conclusion of the novel, Mercier's and Camier's aborted journey (started and stopped throughout the narrative) amounts to one of their many failed attempts to break away from society:

> For needless to say it is townward they are bound, as always when they leave it, as after long vain reckonings the head falls back among the data. (P. 105)

Both the structure of *Mercier and Camier* and several moments within it offer explanations of these subverted expeditions, the most persuasive of which are grounded in aspects of Baudrillard's logic of consumption. The characters' initial journey is halted because a "faint, imploring voice" in their heads drivels "on and off" about their "former lives," urging them back to town in search of a sack they have left behind. Yet upon their arrival both Mercier and Camier become aware that the contents of the sack are "superfluous without exception." During their stay in town, a "great light" bathes their "understanding," revealing the copresence of two "needs": the "need you have" and the "need to have it" (p. 72). Throughout the novel these two needs inevitably enter into conflict, their relative strengths approximating the duo's alternating desires to leave society and to return to town in search of a lost "it." The need for "it" in the particular instance of the sack is historically determined by a faint voice of former social status analogous to the powerful presence of characters' past statuses in Beckett's plays. In sum, the relationship of "need for it"/"need you have" is homologous to the binarism social categorization/"green-world" escape or antistructure. And, as I have maintained above, the one term ("the need you have") operates only as a weaker "satellite" of the stronger (the "need for it").

The narrator of *Mercier and Camier* emphasizes that the "need for it" is not immanent in the material circumstances of the novel's wandering heroes, circumstances not nearly so dire as those of their theatrical counterparts. (Is Malone's need to make an inventory of the objects he possesses any more "necesarry"?) On the contrary, Mercier and Camier's expedition is, in the narrator's estimation, "fairly easy going" physically, and they certainly possess funds sufficient to "keep them going." Yet, of course, they never *keep* going for very long. Why? In part at least, because the country into which they travel both for them and the novel's narrator is saturated with the ideology of the "need for it" which characterizes the logic of consumption. As Baudrillard reminds us, capitalism originates in the Judeo-Christian notion that it is "God's will that Man exploit nature according to his own ends" (*MP,* p. 63). Beckett's narrator hints ironically at the power of this rationale:

> The field lay spread before them. In it nothing grew, that is nothing of use to man. . . . Someday someone would realize [the field's potential]. Then the builders would come. Or a priest, with his sprinkler, and another acre would be God's. When prosperity returned. (P. 54)

Retreating from the field, Mercier and Camier later agree that "contrary to prevalent opinion, there are places in nature from which God would appear to be absent" (p. 72). But throughout the novel, God's presence is equated with the utility of nature; when prosperity returns, nature will be both useful and divinely shaped. (Beckett's biting irony here links "prosperity" with the Church as institution.) Most important, as the sack and its "superfluous" contents intimate, the "need for it" should not be regarded as purely "natural," or essential for survival, but as a desire to possess the signifying values of objects. This need controls Mercier's and Camier's actions, finally making impossible any rupture from the town (and its codes) to which they continually retreat.

Another method of dismantlng the ritual/myth binarism and asserting the preeminence of social determination in *Mercier and Camier* involves the isolation of moments resonant of the green-world myth and its values. Of the many formal repetitions in the novel, one contains moments which resemble the encounter at the barren field mentioned above; namely, the "garden" meetings of Mercier and Camier which open and close the narrative. In the opening meeting, Mercier and Camier convene in Saint Ruth Square, which in fact is not a square but a public garden in the center of town. The square designates, on one level, a green world in which people breathe "more freely" than in town; the garden's pagoda provides shelter from the rain, and the garden itself proves attractive to dogs as a place to copulate. On another level, however, Saint Ruth Square is never free of the Law, as a ranger—one of several constables and other figures of authority with whom Mercier and Camier come into conflict—finally forces the wanderers to leave. The last scene of the novel begins in similarly pastoral fashion by a canal under Lock Bridge on the periphery of town. As they gaze almost rapturously at stars and flowers, Camier asks Mercier about a nearby building and learns that the "grim pile" is actually a hospital for patients suffering from diseases of the skin. As Mercier remarks that there is "not all that howling this evening" from the hospital, we begin to recognize that, much like the Saint Ruth Square and the surrounding countryside, this tiny green world lacks essentiality because it is never separable from social institutions. The possibility of escape is pure mythology. Utility is immanent in the field; Law governs the garden almost as vigilantly as the Church rules William Blake's "Garden of Love"; institutions lurk grimly over green worlds.

In typically Irish fashion, pubs also represent sites of freedom in *Mercier and Camier*. As the narrator explains, it is "in the bars" that Mercier and Camier talk with "greatest freedom, greatest profit." (Here even the term "freedom" becoms perverted by association with "profit.") Like the gardens, public houses are veritable oases in a vast desert of social institutions, laws, and commodities which carry with them a regulating and prohibitive ideology. But for Beckett's heroes every bar has a manager or proprietor—an upholder of the Law of the establishment—with whom Mercier and Camier are sooner or later at odds. And often such disputes center around the pub's inability to satisfy their discriminating tastes,their "need" for delicacies or services appropriate to their sense of social standing. Here their need for "it" collides with the value of the pub as a site of freedom or an avenue of escape, just as the regulating social structure insinuates itself into man's relationship with nature.

The dismantling of the ritual/green-world structure, then, calls into question the relational status of each term as it reveals the superior strength of the social, economic, and ideological components of what I have termed above as "ritual." More important—and I find this to be an especially useful appropriation from Baudrillard's critiques—this dismantling hints at ways in which the "green-world" impulse *itself* serves to aid the social structure in maintaining its dominance. The impulse to escape such structuration, or "need you have," that seems to transcend the world of objects and the ideology attached to them, is itself controlled by regulatory forces manufactured by the very social order one desires to escape. Thus, the narrator's dream of hawthorn and wild roses in "The Expelled," Estragon's reverie of swimming and happiness in the Dead Sea, Nell's fervid memories of Lake Como, or Winnie's gleeful recollection of the back garden at Borough Green might be regarded as fictions serving in collusion with a dominating political economy. The nuclear element of this economy? An object form that is neither pure commodity nor sign, but "indissolubly both" within a code of signification which "never ceases to monitor and systematically control meaning" (*PE,* pp. 148, 150). And this code, before a character steps on stage, is "already" and "always" there.

3. The Political Economy of Objects and Their Ideological Implications

From what moment in all of Beckett's production might one inaugurate a "double" analysis both of the social functions of objects and of their ideological implications? After admitting the capriciousness of the selection, perhaps with Winnie's statement in *Happy Days* that "things have their life"; *things* have a "life" (p. 40), she reiterates to her husband, Willie. But what sort of life? In one respect, the sort of life of the narrator's hat in "The Expelled." The hat, at least as the narrator perceives it, seems to have "pre-existed from time immemorial in a pre-established place," in a more or less permanent order of things. Similarly located and (pre)determined in *Happy Days* is Winnie's indestructable looking-glass:

> I take up this little glass, I shiver it on a stone—*(does so)*—I throw it away—*(does so far behind her)*—it will be in the bag tomorrow, without a scratch, to help me through the day. (P. 30)

Unlike Winnie, who professes a need for her mirror, toothpaste, and other objects, these objects, as she tells Willie, do not need her. Winnie emphasizes both the autonomy of objects and their regulatory power when she concedes that, even though she tries to ignore the bell which awakens her, she cannot deny its powers. So, if objects "help" Winnie through the day (recall here Kenner's notion that objects aid characters by affording them a means of "killing time"),[20] they do so by controlling her in ways of which she is scarcely conscious.

To conduct an inquiry into the sources of this control, we must finally dismiss as a mystifying false lead the materiality of objects and their putative utility. Winnie, in fact, implies that the satisfaction of need resides not in the substantial but in the imaginary when she clarifies her need for Willie:

> Just to know that *in theory* you can hear me even though *in fact* you don't is all I need, just to feel you there within earshot and conceivably on the *qui vive* is all I ask. (P. 22; my emphasis)

That objects and services such as attentiveness satisfy in the realm of the imaginary should not be surprising; this phenomenon is precisely what Baudrillard, borrowing from the Lacanian conception of the *stade du miroir,* attacks as the logic of consumption. (And, in Winnie's case, Lacan's insistence that the human subject and subjectivity tend toward the fictional, the mirror image, is especially revealing.)[21] More broadly, as Cornelius Castoriadis avers, society inevitably transforms so-called "natural" facts into signifying constructs. The rationale of this transformation cannot be deduced simply through scrutiny of the "fact." Take, for instance, the "natural" fact of gender:

> But if the latter [the institution of society] must allow for the *natural fact* of being-male and being-female, institution involves the transformation of this fact into an *imaginary social signification* of being-a-man or being-a-woman. . . . Everything that, in one way or another, is apprehended or perceived by society must *signify* something or be invested with a signification, and what is more, it not only signifies, but is always apprehended in advance of and by the possibility of signification. (*SA.* Pp. 33, 39)

Once one accedes to the notion that Winnie is *not* beyond society, that her consciousness *has* been integrated into a larger network of values and systems of encoding, then the identity of objects, services, and need in *Happy Days* is defined by this network. Winnie's all-important bag is invested with myriad significations, ones which are foregrounded in act 2 because of her inability to use any object in its materiality. For example, the bag signifies constancy and enduring presence. Even after Willie is gone, she speculates, "there will always be the bag." Near the end of the play, Winnie suggests other significations:

> The bag too is there, the same as ever. I can see it. *(Pause. Eyes right. Louder.)* The bag is there, Willie, as good as ever, the one you gave me that day . . . to go to market. (P. 38)

Thus, while the bag *does* possess *some* degree of utility—it holds Winnie's precious few possessions—it more importantly signifies, among other things, Willie's affection for his wife or his valorization of her role as hauler of goods from the market. In another respect, the bag's value is analogous to Willie's in that his "real" existence, much like the bag's, becomes less important than Winnie's convenient fiction of his presence:

> I say I used to think I would learn to talk alone. *(Pause.)* By that I mean to myself, the wilderness. *(Smile.)* But no. *(Smiler broader.)* No no. *(Smile off.)* Ergo you are there. *(Pause.)* Oh no doubt you are dead, like

the others, no doubt you have died, or gone away and left me, like the
others, it doesn't matter, you are there. (Pp. 37–38)

What I am proposing here is that act 2 of *Happy Days,* because in it any
sense of an object's utility is exploded by Winnie's immobility and consequent inability to "use" anything, betrays the fetishized nature of all
objects in Beckett's plays. As Baudrillard explains, in the "fetishist"
theory consumption is dictated by an object's participation in a "regulated
play of signifiers," *not* by the utility of the signified:

> In the "fetishist" theory of consumption . . . objects are given and
> received everywhere as force dispensers (happiness, health, security,
> prestige, etc.). This magical substance having been spread about so
> liberally, one forgets that what we are dealing with first are signs: a
> generalized code of signs, a totally arbitrary code of difference, *and that
> it is on this basis, and not at all on account of their use values or their
> innate "virtues," that objects exercise their fascination.* (*PE.* P. 91;
> Baudrillard's emphasis)

Winnie, like all of us in one way or another, is dazzled by the code,
fascinated with and satisfied by signification.

In *Happy Days,* the "generalized code of signs" perpetuates Winnie's
vivid romantic fantasies; her few possessions represent socially produced
notions of being a woman. Both fantasies and normalizing conceptions of
womanhood are registered by objects in the play, the latter most strikingly
evident in Winnie's attire and Beckett's description of her as feminine
object:

> Embedded up to her waist [in act 1] in exact centre of mound, WINNIE.
> About fifty, well-preserved blonde for preference, plump, arms and
> shoulders bare, low bodice, big bosom, pearl necklace. (P. 9)

Winnie's somewhat formal attire matches Willie's top hat, morning coat,
and white gloves—his costume which Beckett characterizes through the
cliché "dressed to kill." But what in Beckett's description of Willie corresponds to being "well preserved" or possessing a "big bosom" or blonde
hair? And why the bare arms and shoulders, the partial nudity inherent in
codes of women's formal attire? Perhaps more significant than the existence of this code is Winnie's gleeful acceptance of it, as evinced by her
reliance upon beauty "aids" and her nostalgia for the past. (One might
note here that Winnie's revolver, displayed prominently but never fired, is
never fired in part because it exists outside the code of being-a-woman in
which Winnie is ensnared.) Ostensibly more mature than, say, Gerty
MacDowell in James Joyce's *Ulysses,* Winnie is imprisoned within a code
of beauty and caught in a web of romantic fantasy similar to those which

enslave her younger Dublin predecessor.[22] Winnie swigs medicine adver-
tised to promote "instantaneous improvement"; she brandishes a stylish
parasol which, like her bag, Willie gave her for "that day" on the lake
(indeed, Willie and men appear to have given her everything, including her
consciousness); she sings to a "musical box" tune lyrics extolling an
idealized love and happier days for her when Willie "came whining" for
her hand declaring his worship:

> Every touch of fingers
> Tells me what I know,
> Says for you,
> It's true, it's true,
> You love me so!

(P. 47)

The subtleties of this lyric replicate the process of signification in Beckettian objects. That is, for Winnie the touch (a variety of constituting "gaze"
or "look") not only signifies love, but also reiterates a totally imagined
signified, something of which she claims *a priori* knowledge. The touch
itself has no clear or univocal meaning outside of the imaginary, just as
objects in *Happy Days* have no inherent "virtue" or utility. But the touch
speaks for the subject; its deployment "says" what Winnie wants to hear
in the same language as that articulated upon the articles in her bag.[23]

In this way, then, Mercier's and Camier's confident postulation of two
separate needs—the "need for it" and the "need you have"—is symp-
tomatic of a delusive simplification (rationalization) in Beckett's plays. Or,
perhaps more accurately, plays such as *Happy Days* intimate the extent to
which the "need for it" is in actuality a need for a fetishized object and its
rich significative value. If so, then characters' desires to break from society
should be revalued with especial attention paid to the way in which such
desires aid in the maintenance of a fetishized consumption. The "need you
have"—one which I have conflated with the network of allusions in Beckett's drama to a "green-world" transcendence—can thus be recognized as
a comparatively puny satellite of the need for it. More important, the
"green-world" moment in Beckett's plays effects a temporary displacement from the "it" which serves finally to reinvest the it—the object—
with more power and attractiveness than it possessed before such temporary flights. The "inexorable domain of the quotidian real" (Francis Barker's phrase, used in a vastly different context) in Beckett's plays is
therefore not only definable as a depressed material or physical real: the
so-called "real" importantly includes imaginary components familiar to all
of us.[24]

I might conclude by suggesting that Baudrillard's more recent consid-
erations of simulation in postmodern society—ones which expand his

critique of theories of need or utility in analyzing consumption—may have quite accidentally led him to the theater of Samuel Beckett. Especially in *In the Shadow of the Silent Majorities,* Baudrillard describes what might very well be an apt characterization of Beckett's gallery of dramatis personae: the "mass." Baudrillard explains:

> The "peasant masses" of old were not in fact masses: only those form a mass who are freed from their symbolic bondage, "released" (only to be caught in infinite "networks") and destined to be no more than the innumerable end points of precisely those same theoretical models which do not succeed in integrating them and finally only produce them as statistical refuse. . . . It [the mass] has nothing to do with any *real* population, body or specific social aggregate. (*SM.* P. 5)

But the "mass" survives, consuming voraciously to achieve status or prestige. To be sure, Baudrillard's "mass" is in *no way* conflatable with or convertible into a model of Beckett's characters or a précis of his politics. It does, however, bring to the foreground a source of endurance in Beckett which is, paradoxically, *the* source of stasis also: the "glaring impossibility of an autonomous change in consciousness" (*SM,* p. 30). If for nothing else than his relentless exploration of this impossibility—and his demystification of the fictions, many of which are represented by seemingly impregnable binarisms, we employ to conceal it—Beckett is a responsible political writer.

Notes

1. Samuel Beckett, *Waiting for Godot* (New York: Grove Press, 1954), p. 7r. Each number is used for the recto and verso side of a page; hence "r" is used for recto, "v" for verso. All further references to Beckett's work will be cited by page number from this and the following editions and will be included in the text: *Three Novels by Samuel Beckett: Molloy, Malone Dies, The Unnamable* (New York: Grove Press, 1955), *Endgame* (New York: Grove Press, 1957), *Krapp's Last Tape and Other Dramatic Pieces* (New York: Grove Press, 1957), *Happy Days* (London: Faber and Faber, 1963); *Mercier and Camier* (New York: Grove Press, 1974); "The Expelled," in *I Can't Go On, I'll Go On,* ed. Richard W. Seaver (New York: Grove Press, 1976); and *Three Occasional Pieces* (London: Faber and Faber, 1983).
2. See Georg Lukács, *The Meaning of Contemporary Realism,* trans. John and Necke Mander (London: Merlin Press, 1962), especially pp. 17–46. In his critique of Franz Kafka, Lukács alleges that, like Kafka's, Beckett's treatment of "abstract particularity" prevents him from "investing observed detail with typical significance." Consequently, Beckett has "emptied everyday life of meaning" (p. 45). Terry Eagleton seemingly endorses Lukács's position on Beckett and other "bourgeois modernists" in *Marxism and Literary Criticism* (Berkeley and Los Angeles: University of California Press, 1976), pp. 27–31. For a political reading of Beckett, see Darko Suvin, "Preparing for Godot—or the Purgatory of Individualism," *Tulane Drama Review,* 11 (Summer 1967): 23–36. See also Thomas Cousineau, "*Waiting for Godot* and Politics," in *Coriolan: Théâtre et Politique,* eds. Jean-Paul

Debax and Yves Peyré (Toulouse: Université de Toulouse-Le Mirail, 1984), pp. 161–67.

3. John Fekete, *The Critical Twilight* (London: Routledge and Kegan Paul, 1977), pp. 217–18. I shall also quote from Fekete's collection of essays, *The Structural Allegory: Reconstructive Encounters with the New French Thought* (Minneapolis: University of Minnesota Press, 1983). All further references to *The Structural Allegory,* abbreviated *SA,* will be cited by page number and included in the text.

4. Hugh Kenner, *Samuel Beckett: A Critical Study* (Berkeley and Los Angeles: University of California Press, 1969), p. 142.

5. Here I refer to Arnold van Gennep, *The Rites of Passage,* trans. Monika B. Vizedom and Gabrielle L. Caffee (Chicago: University of Chicago Press, 1966); Victor Turner, *The Ritual Process* (Ithaca: Cornell University Press, 1969), especially pp. 94–130; and Turner, *Dramas, Fields, and Metaphors* (Ithaca N.Y.: Cornell University Press, 1974), pp. 23–59. All further references to Turner's works, abbreviated *RP* and *DFM* respectively and followed by page numbers, will be included in the text.

6. S.E. Gontarski, *The Intent of Undoing in Samuel Beckett's Dramatic Texts* (Bloomington: Indiana University Press, 1985), p. 173. While most of this essay was written—and a version of it read at the 1984 convention of the Modern Language Association—before Gontarski's book was published, I find his discussion of the functioning of the "green world" in Beckett compatible with my own. Gontarski emphasizes, correctly I think, that Didi, Hamm, Krapp, Winnie, and others "long for an age that has vanished, or perhaps never existed. Against the background of god, fertility, love, those traces, memories, or fabrications of individuals and their culture, Beckett foregrounds his hellish, shifting, capricious dramas" (p. 173). And I agree with his occasionally enunciated, though never developed, Derridean and Lacanian reading of the plays' lack of both centers and absolute subjects. I wish only to consider this "green world" and its implications in more detail, in the process demonstrating the status of this world as something much more than a botanical "background."

7. Northrop Frye, *Anatomy of Criticism* (Princeton: Princeton University Press, 1957), p. 182.

8. *As you Like It,* act 2, sc. 1, lines 1–5.

9. Vivian Mercier, *Beckett/Beckett* (New York: Oxford University Press, 1977), p. 56.

10. Annis Pratt, "Women and Nature in Modern Fiction," *Contemporary Literature,* 13 (1972): 476.

11. Simone de Beauvoir, *The Second Sex* (New York: Knopf, 1953), as quoted by Pratt, p. 477.

12. Mercier, p. 47.

13. René Girard, *Violence and the Sacred,* trans. Patrick Gregory (Baltimore: Johns Hopkins University Press, 1977), p. 284.

14. Girard, p. 280.

15. I borrow the metaphors "host" and "parasite" from J. Hillis Miller, "The Critic as Host" in *Deconstruction and Criticism* (New York: Seabury Press, 1979), pp. 217–53. That Beckett deconstructs binary opposites or probes an aporia that undoes seemingly concrete pairings is hardly news to readers of Beckett. As J. D. O'Hara observes about *Malone Dies,* "If we attempt to define this two-sidedness [in the novel] we realize that it can never clearly be perceived—partly because the terms on each side elude definition and partly because they are not completely separable" (p. 64). See "About Structure in *Malone Dies,*" in *Twentieth Century Interpretations of Molloy, Malone Dies, The Unnamable,* ed. J. D. O'Hara (Englewood Cliffs, N.J.: Prentice-Hall, 1970), pp. 62–70. If this is so—and Malone's

clear repudiations of pairs such as hot/cold, food/excrement, dish/pot, and need/
want suggest that it is—then the binarism myth/ritual is similarly unstable. The
"green world," garden, or nature in Beckett can never be free of social axiom or
regulation. In *Malone Dies* this is represented by the Saposcats, whose lives were
"full of axioms" (p. 187). Sapo "loved nature" and would "stand rapt" in admiration of it, while his father imposes regulations in the maintenance of the family
garden and is primarily concerned with the high cost of such maintenance.

16. Of course, the lack of a concrete spatio-temporal matrix in a fictive text need
not suggest a concomitant lack of social or political meaning. Several plays of
Edward Bond, for example, contain powerful and relevant critiques of class structure, capitalism, and the like without specifying an exact or concrete historical
target.

17. Lukács, p. 37.

18. This topic was discussed in a special session ("Ritual Patterns in Samuel
Beckett's Plays") at the MLA Convention, Washington, 27–30 December 1984. As
a participant in this session, I am indebted to its organizer Katherine H. Burkman,
who read an earlier draft of this essay, and to Susan Brienza and Lois More
Overbeck for their insights into ritual in Beckett.

19. Jean Baudrillard, *For a Critique of the Political Economy of the Sign,* trans.
Charles Levin and Arthur Younger (St. Louis: Telos Press, 1981), p. 29. All further
references to this text, abbreviated *PE,* will be cited by page number and included
in the text. All references to Baudrillard's *The Mirror of Production,* trans. Mark
Poster (St. Louis: Telos Press, 1974), abbreviated *MP,*—and to Baudrillard's *In the
Shadow of the Silent Majorities,* trans. Paul Foss, Paul Patton, and John Johnston
(New York: Semiotext(e), 1983), abbreviated *SM*—will be similarly cited in the
text. For a helpful bibliography of works by and on Baudrillard, see John Fekete's
The Structural Allegory, pp. 251–52. For a discussion of Baudrillard's work and his
attack on Foucault, see Karlis Racevskis, "The Theoretical Violence of a Cata-
strophical Strategy," *Diacritics,* 9 (September 1979): 33–42.

20. Kenner, p. 142.

21. See Jacques Lacan, "Le stade du miroir comme formateur de la fonction du
Je," in *Écrits* (Paris: Editions du Seuil, 1966), pp. 93–100.

22. See Suzette A. Henke, *Joyce's Moraculous Sindbook* (Columbus: Ohio
State University Press, 1978), pp. 153–79. Here Henke explores the origins of
Gerty MacDowell's consciousness in popular romantic novels and the "beauty"
sections of women's magazines. In many respects, the lame Gerty MacDowell's
fantasies and values are analogous to the immobile Winnie's. Another component
of the horizon which Winnie cannot transcend is intimated by her numerous
allusions to canonically "high" literature: Shakespeare, Milton, Keats, Browning,
and so on. This issue has been discussed numerous times, but seldom as a
component of a dominant formation which controls Winnie. See, for example,
James Knowlson, "Beckett's Bits of Pipe," in *Samuel Beckett: Humanistic Perspectives,* eds. Morris Beja, S. E. Gontarski, and Pierre Astier (Columbus: Ohio
State University Press, 1982), pp. 16–25. Last, one might regard Winnie's entrapment as emblematic both of women's confinement in a patriarchal society and
women's status as art-object. For an especially interesting discussion of this, see
Susan Gubar, "'The Blank Page' and the Issues of Female Creativity," *Critical
Inquiry,* 8 (Winter 1981): 243–63.

23. In a recent article—"Seeing is Believing: Baudrillard and Blau," *Theatre
Journal,* 37 (May 1985): 141–54—Patricia Mellencamp cites Baudrillard's comment that the contemporary subject, wallowing in unremitting hyperreality, is "no
longer produced as mirror, but pure screen" (p.144). Mellencamp helpfully observes that for Baudrillard the "problem or crime is the imaginary," which has all
of us and all of Beckett's characters in its hold. Beckett's Malone, we might recall,

emphasizes that *"Nothing is more real than nothing"* (p. 192). If so, then most everything else is to a greater or lesser degree imaginary, less "real." While not so glaring as, say, the hyperreality of Disney World or the California tourist traps explored by Umberto Eco in *Travels in Hyperreality* (New York: Harcourt Brace Jovanovich, 1986), the "realities" fabricated by Beckett's characters are, albeit less spectacular, similarly unauthentic.

24. Francis Barker, *The Tremulous Private Body: Essays in Subjection* (London: Methuen, 1984), p. 5.

Bad Habits While Waiting for Godot

The Demythification of Ritual

Claudia Clausius

Embracing a friend, quarreling, sitting down, talking to a stranger, looking at a tree—these actions are not usually considered rituals. What promotes the mundane habits and conventions in Samuel Beckett's *Waiting for Godot* to the status of ritual is Didi's and Gogo's motivation in using them and the unique function these perform in the tramps' daily lives. In the play Beckett demonstrates that the tramps' conscious manipulation of ritual leads to self-parody, which undermines the efficacy of ritual in contemporary life. Traditionally, parody first assumes a familiarity and an intimacy with the audience before it proceeds with its real purpose of exposure. Beckett's parody of ritual, however, is richer and more complex than this. Directly influenced by Charles Chaplin's parody of ritual in his comic films, Beckett is not content merely to expose ritual; he intends to lay bare the entire social and theatrical machinery of life. Through his use of Chaplinesque characters, Beckett is able to defamiliarize for his characters and for the audience the rituals which comprise everyday life. Commenting on Beckett's use of tramps and clowns, Geneviève Serreau calls this parodic role one of "demystification." "In *Godot* the sacred monster that must be demystified is simply man."[1] More accurately, however, Beckett is concerned with demythification, with exposing myths such as religion, language, love, logic, philosophy, science—in other words, ritualized thought and consciousness.

Traditionally and fundamentally dealing with men and with their gods, ritual bridges the gap between man's reality in this world and his fears of and aspirations for the next. But future-oriented though it is, and fashioned as it may be out of man's hopes, ritual stems entirely from this world and is infused with all the imperfections and limitations of man's nature. While scanning the horizon for Godot, the tramps must still contend with their fellowmen, their own discomforts, and the world around them. They try, for example, to placate Pozzo, to keep Lucky from running amuck, and they "do the tree"—all activities that are basically "for . . . [mental] balance."[2] Their hopes may be mystical, but their reality remains social and worldly. Ritual, then, grounds man on earth—lending support and deflecting anxiety. Eliade states that all those writers for whom myth is subordinate to ritual "tacitly take for granted that the primary and the fundamental element . . . of human culture, is the act done by man, not the story of divine activity."[3] In this respect it is not surprising that Godot never appears. As the well-oiled machinery of society, ritual operates in man's human life. Man may live forever in the next world, or be reincarnated endlessly, but this neither obliterates nor accelerates his time on earth. Should Godot's arrival on the morrow be certain, the tramps would still be faced with today—and with each other.

If ritual attempts to bridge the vacuum between the heavens and this world and the spaces between people on earth, its primary purpose must be to communicate. The communication in ritual is best understood from its verbal and substantive derivatives "to commune" and "the community." The specific ritual works most powerfully on an audience recognizing and sharing in the actions and beliefs represented by the ritual. Thus, ritual's unique type of communication is based upon and directed towards, not understanding, but recognition. Unconcerned with the quest for knowledge, ritual is rooted in the bond of foreknowledge among its participants. In *Waiting for Godot* Beckett, through a series of plays-within-a-play, dramatizes his view of existence to an audience participating in both the theatrical and the human (life) experiences exemplified on stage.

This bond of recognition, moreover, must be strong enough to sustain the tension and strain of its connective function. As Max Gluckman states, all social interaction, including all communication, must involve potentially dangerous tension among its disparate participants. He asserts that ritual, in establishing a common and accepted mode of behavior, successfully resolves such conflict through the "juxtaposition and overlapping of functionally distinct roles."[4] Although one enters the realm of drama when roles are assigned and recognized, man cannot forever be on stage, subsisting on the cues and lines of a given role. Man may, indeed, succeed in avoiding conflict during the ritual, but unless life becomes one long extended ritual, the inevitable moment must come when he confronts conflict and tension. By manipulating the popular analogy between society and theater, Beckett demonstrates the inherent deficiencies and limits of social ritual.

The dialectical tension between the structure of ritual and its content is also one of its most elementary characteristics. The participants' foreknowledge refers to both a knowledge and acceptance of their specific roles in the drama and a profound intimacy with the drama's inherent incomprehensibility. The reenactment of ritual, therefore, is only a dance around a content which consistently eludes it. Far from offering answers, ritual reiterates the questions, indeed emphasizes their inscrutability. In this way ritual constitutes the vocabulary of the language of incomprehensibility. Beneath the apparent sense of the words and ideas communicated during ritual exists a subtext whose power asserts itself arbitrarily but consistently in the minds of the participants, leaving them with nothing more than the need to reenact the ritual in order to escape their bewilderment at existence.

Escape is not always possible given the cyclical tendency both of ritual and of life, and the degree to which these two activities reflect and draw upon one another. Often while in the midst of ritual the two tramps put an end to their skits by inadvertently stumbling onto precisely those dangers they had wished to evade: waiting and thinking. Describing conventional ritual, Georges Gusdorf speaks of the "sleep of mythical immobility" and the "captivity of participation."[5] Furthermore, not only their consciousness of ritual, but also their friendship toward one another keeps them alive to their real purpose of waiting for Godot. Didi refuses to let Gogo fall asleep and in a wider sense both tramps keep each other awake to their common reality.

The tramps' reliance on ritual is stressed particularly in act 1, the act in which Beckett sets the scene for the final demythification of ritual in act 2. The Pozzo and Lucky of act 1 are disqualified as equal partners for the tramps because their lives have become unthinkingly routine. Communication with Lucky is about as likely as conversation with an animal. Furthermore, Pozzo's ceaseless acting reveals itself as an unsatisfactory alternative to the tramps' lethargy and anxiety. By acting, Pozzo forces people to watch him, so that his function becomes that of performing. This theatrical escape, however, is impossible for the philosopher and the poet of the drama, whose roles in the ritual evolve dramatically throughout the play.

There are noticeably fewer instances of ritual in act 2, and what skits do occur are less prolonged and therefore also less parodic. As the act progresses the tramps change from participants to spectators, their acting relying more on soliloquy than on dialogue. The prominent "action" of the second act is watching and discussing Pozzo's moves and cries for help. His pleas of "Pity! Pity!" (p. 53v) annoy the tramps to the point of violence as Didi strikes Pozzo and then calmly watches as the blind man crawls away. Both Didi's words and posture suggest his exclusion from participation:

> VLADIMIR: (. . . *Vladimir, propped on his elbow, observes his* [Pozzo's]
> *retreat.*) He's off! (*Pozzo collapses.*) He's down!
> (Pp. 53v–54r)

Even the jargon underscores his commentator and spectator roles. He describes first a horse racing event and secondly a boxing match, both "theatrical" rituals involving participants and spectators. In his sporting metaphors, moreover, Didi, like Gloucester before him in *King Lear,* intimates that human suffering is a sport for the gods or, in terms of the play, for Godot and for us.

Didi in act 2 echoes Pozzo's words in act 1, and within the second act the two characters again echo each other. In the midst of his pitiful suffering, Pozzo's poetry seems to suggest a glimmer of enlightenment: "When! When! One day, is that not enough for you . . . They give birth astride of a grave, the light gleams an instant, then it's night once more" (p. 58r). Not long after this Didi takes his cue from Pozzo's exit lines and elaborates on them:

> VLADIMIR: Astride of a grave and a difficult birth. Down in the hole, lingeringly, the grave-digger puts on the forceps. We have time to grow old. The air is full of our cries.
>
> (Pp. 58v–59r)

He ends with the conclusion: "But habit is a great deadener" and then asks himself, "What have I said?" (p. 59r). All his play acting, all his deliberate or unintentional mimicking of Pozzo have at least led him to this epiphany. Scarcely able to bear the import of his words, he moves about feverishly and then broods alone at the far left of the stage. But to participate is at least to do and, when the Boy enters, Didi realizes he must begin the ritual again.

Ritual, then, is born precisely because the responsibilities incumbent upon knowledge and freedom are too frightening, so much so that, faced even with the loss of the original belief in ritual, man continues to find solace in its reenactment. Both tramps suspect that Godot will never keep his appointment ("Off we go again," pp. 32v, 59r), but in self-defense they accept, indeed foster, the cyclicity of existence.

If the participants recognize quite clearly the epistemological emptiness of the ritual, some reason must explain their continued reenactment of the nonfunctional rites. Margaret Mead makes a nice observation by implicitly pointing to the distinction between ritual and ritual behavior: "Throughout human history man has employed ritual behavior to deal with critical moments."[6] Man seeks refuge in the behavior, in the acting out of the ritual, not so much in the ritual itself, as if in the face of noncomprehension he finds comfort in activity (as opposed to action), in an unthinking repetition that carries itself and its participants along with it.

Ritual involves a "looking forward to"—an expectation and an anticipation—emotions which glean their momentum from the past by pushing the present forcefully into the future. But the repetition of ritual disarms and eventually usurps the rational and unique emotional life of the participants to the point at which the ritual controls them more than they control it. If ritual simultaneously represents a history of belief and an anticipation of salvation, a glancing back and a searching ahead, it may eventually become a vicious circle leading around itself, being both center and circumference.

As the hope of Godot's future arrival turns into the reality of the day that has passed, optimistic expectation changes into bitter experience. As soon as the tramps' faith becomes a precedent, they learn to expect and to accept more of the same. Their ritual, however, is more than form without content or repetition without belief. In parody, the form and repetition are the content. The ritual leads nowhere but back to itself, to the need for more ritual; it no longer links man with his origins in the past and his merits in the future. Paradoxically, even when emptied of its original role and promise, ritual then functions as consolation to mitigate the purpose it no longer serves. The crisis now is that contact between myth and ritual no longer exists; man is cut off and alone. Ritual now becomes a means unto itself without which life is intolerable. The inheritance from the past and the prophecy for the future implicit in ritual unite, becoming one and the same thing in an eternal present of the gerundial mode—waiting.

The strain of waiting consistently prompts the tramps into ritual, often in order to avoid "thought." Willingly putting his critical and reasoning consciousness in abeyance during ritual, man allows the "primitive" inheritance of his ancestors (their faith in the ritual) a temporary victory. After discovering that Pozzo is blind, Gogo hopefully suggests: "Perhaps he can see into the future" (p. 55r)—that is, can see when Godot will appear. The legendary connection between blindness and prophecy comprises part of Gogo's intellectual inheritance, one which pushes itself to the forefront when an event occurs in the real world recalling the possibility of truth. The pure arbitrariness of the inexplicable event (Pozzo's blindness) evokes a sudden hope within Gogo and revives this ancient faith's ambiguous potential. In other words, Gogo is momentarily prepared to believe in Pozzo's visionary powers precisely because he has been struck blind. In this way the past rituals, whose ancient forms are preserved within the mind of man, forever conform to the present realities man must confront. Paradoxically, however, ritual's ability to conform is indiscriminate in judging its congruence with circumstance, and thus it often leads itself into self-parody. Part of the hilarity of Gogo's suggestion is the parody to which he unwittingly subjects his own infantile hope.

In his play Beckett mocks the "myth" (the announced and awaited messiah Godot) through the tramps' comically condensed, picaresque tour of the various ritualized institutions of contemporary society. The social conventions, the habits of language and thought, the plays-within-a-play echoing dramatic and literary traditions—all these elements, by comprising the ritual of the tramps' and our daily lives, and by setting it in a parodic light, reflect the human condition at the same time as they offer insight into it. Indeed, ordinary habits and conventions assume the intensity of ritual for the tramps precisely because they need these to "get through the day." Paradoxically, the tramps make use of the rituals at the same time as they are aware of their futility and impotence; they "demythify" themselves even as they act as creators or perpetuators of myth. They recognize that reenacting a structured emptiness is still preferable to living a formless void. The parody to which Didi and Gogo subject the rituals mitigates their bitter recognition because it places them in control. Using the inherent limitations of ritual, they gain an intellectual victory over what would otherwise be mere automatism.

Watching the tramps, we see ourselves. This mirror/window effect is most obvious when the tramps and Pozzo watch Lucky "perform"; at two removes we see the characters watching what we perceive to be a parody. If Lucky is an unconscious vehicle, however, Didi and Gogo are painfully aware of their manipulations of convention and of their acting roles—a crucial recognition which places the function of pretension and theatricality at the center of the drama.

Christopher Innes in his discussion of ritual and avant-garde drama remarks that Beckett "stresses artificiality rather than 'noble artifice'" and adds "hence too the self-conscious music-hall jokes that remind us this is only theatre."[7] However, when Gogo calls to Didi out in the wings, "End of the corridor, on the left," and when Didi responds, "Keep my seat" (p. 24r), Beckett does not intend to deprecate theater, but to stress the similarities between theater and life, to reveal indeed that life is theater, is ritual. The artificiality becomes ennobled through a recognition of the artifice. Didi consciously lives the fine line between life and theater: "But it is not for nothing I have lived through this long day and I can assure you it is very near the end of its repertory" (p. 55v). The mention of "repertory" is particularly apt in its suggestion of a permanent company (mankind) performing an established set of dramatic works (social rituals).

What we are faced with in *Waiting for Godot* are several interdependent "theatrical arenas": first, the drama (as a live presentation of speech and action in two acts) is obviously theater; secondly, the skits which constitute the play also represent theater; thirdly, both the structure and the content of the piece—the parody—allude to the actual ritual(s) of life's drama; and finally, since the lifeblood of parody comes from an external appreciation of its references to previous tradition, the actors and the audience become involved as participants in a parodic rite that presupposes a common past in which the original traditions were practiced with gravity and belief. If Beckett intends to manipulate artifice to unmask artifice and to leave us with the essential reality, his first task must be to confront the theatricality of all these aspects. This confrontation achieves the defamiliarization. Having reestablished in our minds the "ritual" in all human activity and endeavor, Beckett then proceeds to strip away the pretension to reveal the truth and to demythify man.

But to break the implicit "fourth wall" of ritual presents enormous difficulties because all aspects of human life have become ritualized to the point at which the ritual is often mistaken for the "thing in itself" or the reality. By granting ritual theatrical integrity, that fourth wall is rebuilt which separates ritual from reality. If ritual, a genre of theater, has de-throned reality, it is only by subjecting it to artifice in the form of another convention that one can extract it from reality. And what better means of achieving this than within a formalized convention in which the artifice comprises part of the basic structure of the ritual.

"Inspiring prospects" (p. 10v), despairs Gogo near the beginning of the play as he surveys the audience. In the second act, Didi, trying to reassure his friend and pointing into the auditorium declares: "There! Not a soul in sight!" (p. 48r). The self-references in *Waiting for Godot* draw attention to the plays-within-a-play and to the larger drama which exists as part of the tradition of theater. But since theater deliberately sets out to "make believe," this kind of "alienation" or defamiliarization device undercuts the theater's function, apparently leaving the drama bereft of purpose or intent. Destroying this particular theatrical convention, however, is part of Beckett's artistic and philosophic design. The actors on stage momentarily drop their roles to wink at the audience. The entire theatrical experience—in conventional terms, that of the actors and that of the audience—is undermined. The audience is repeatedly implicated in Didi's and Gogo's bewilderment and despair at their stagnant and lifeless appointment site:

VLADIMIR: *(Looking round):* You recognize the place?
ESTRAGON: I didn't say that.

. . . .

VLADIMIR: All the same . . . that tree . . . *(turning towards auditorium)* that bog . . .

(P. 11r)

By virtue of its presence in the theater, the audience keeps the tramps company during their wait.

The skits within the larger play parody the rituals which they represent and which inspire them. In this way they also parody the theatrical structure within which they exist. When Pozzo demands from the tramps, "A little attention, if you please" (p. 25r), we feel guilty, as though our own concentration had been noticeably flagging. We take our place on stage in a sense. Beckett's emphasis on the artifice of his drama works against theatrical convention in the service of parody and he achieves a paring away of layers of artifice within a traditionally recognized and accepted artifice—the theater. Once the theatrical ritual from both sides of the footlights and all the institutions reflected therein are stripped of their "gesture," one final rite survives which has consistently raised its head throughout all the distractions. Waiting remains the final core of reality beneath all the layers of ritual: "The essential doesn't change" (p. 15r).

Using the stage to parody theater is not merely Beckett's way of illustrating his ideas in dramatic terms. If the rituals contained within the play undermine the validity of the theater, the theater itself, now the subordinate ritual, undermines the validity of the drama of life. Whether they are played out under the sun or under floodlights, the rites do not change. Parody, however, exposes the machinery beneath the ritual by temporarily suspending its context.

Everyone has at some time seen a group of people gathered together in an elevator. Everybody waits for the doors to close; after a while all eyes look upwards to where the floor numbers are illuminated; then everyone's head turns to the floor selection panel. Meanwhile people outside notice the awkwardness of the people confined in a small space waiting for an event to happen which does not happen. Those inside the elevator become aware that they are being observed and, suddenly self-conscious, become anxious that the elevator should close and move on to the next floor. Ridiculousness and embarrassment are created because the waiting momentarily loses its context and the machinery (in the present instance this works literally) of the ritual is disclosed because it is defective. Because something is not working to expectation, the entire event loses its context and becomes absurd.

Or imagine someone walking purposefully up to the door of a house, knocking, waiting expectantly. Nothing happens; he knocks again, more forcefully. Still no one appears. Waiting, he looks toward the houses on either side, glances down at his shoes, up at the eaves. He may even peer in through the door window. Experiencing acute discomfiture, the person also shortly begins to feel inexplicably culpable. Anyone watching finds him ridiculous, as though he himself were responsible for his absurd predicament. It is not long before he walks quickly back toward the road.

In both instances the rite of waiting only appears sensible as long as its aim is clear. The reason for the waiting must always overshadow the actual waiting. The moment the activity of waiting eclipses its own purpose or goal it becomes absurd.

When the tramps allude to their own role-playing within Beckett's drama and within their own skits, they destroy the context they have created and remind themselves and the audience of their primary mission—waiting. Significantly, the parody surrounding the waiting and giving it substance is the very element which deflates it and renders it futile. Whenever the tramps remember their sojourn, the substance of the parody disappears because it has proven itself defective or rather ineffective.

Nevertheless, the tramps continue seeking to numb their consciousness of the endless waiting in the routine, in the habitual, in convention, and in tradition; they discuss theology and history, imagine tepid honeymoons, pretend to quarrel as lovers; they contemplate suicide and play at being gentlemen. Beckett has described life as a "succession of habits, since the individual is a succession of individuals. . . ."[8] Much like music-hall and circus comedy, the tramps' impromptu skits resemble a series of parodic plays-within-a-play in which they represent the actors. In their various roles they cover a broad range of recognizable "types"—of behavior, of people, of thinking. In this way the tramps represent Everyman as Everyone.

The rich diversity of the tramp character resides in the fact that generically he can emerge from any social, cultural, or academic world, thus presenting the ideal vehicle for parody. The most renowned tramp was, of course, Charlie Chaplin's tramp. The linguistic connection between Chaplin's French nickname, Charlot, and Beckett's Godot suggests an interesting parallel between the film tramp and the stage tramps, Didi and Gogo. The several diminutives set the tone for the parody in the play and alert us to its significance. Both Beckett and Chaplin are concerned with exposure through parody; Chaplin's comic tool was the classic silent film gag, which significantly influenced Beckett's own comic parody. The workings of Chaplin's and Beckett's comedy involve a process of exposure or defamiliarization, which prepares the way for the final demythification of all human ritual.

Czech dramatist Václav Havel has written a fascinating analysis entitled "The Anatomy of the Gag" in which he examines the classic silent film gag's internal structure.[9] In the film *The Idle Class* (1920), the inebriated rich husband, Charlie, receives the news that his wife has left him. Turning his back to us he supports himself on the furniture, weeps and shakes with grief. Then as he slowly turns back towards us we see he is mixing a gin fizz. Havel notes two distinct phases to the gag: 1) Charlie shaking with grief; 2) Charlie mixing a cocktail. The intersection of their logical paths is the point of absurdity. Havel distinguishes these two phases by their active or passive function within the comic structure. The first phase is the "given situation"; it is passive because it must wait to be defamiliarized and rendered absurd by the active second phase which "denies . . . upsets and negates" the previous phase (p. 15). The first phase, Charlie crying, is defamiliarized by the second phase, the gin fizz. In essence what we are dealing with here are really two separate conventions. The real target of defamiliarization is automatism or convention. Both the grief and the cocktail contain elements of automatism; one action, the gin fizz, accurately reflects Charlie's desires while the other action, the crying, remains a mere convention. Havel notes that the first phase (the grief) dehumanizes the character because it stresses convention at the expense of honesty. Contrarily, the automatism or convention of the second phase humanizes since it reflects the character's real desires. The comic absurdity of the gag arises from the process of defamiliarization which it evokes in the spectator.

Havel, summarizing Victor Shklovskii's and Václav Cerný's theories, describes the two essential characteristics of the defamiliarization process as it concerns the spectator or the audience. First, the spectator ceases to perceive the stage action as a performance or as an aesthetic ritual. The roles of the characters in the plot fall away, revealing only actors and scenery. The performance, stripped of its ritualistic trappings is thus reduced to its "factual substance" (p. 14). Secondly, since the spectator no longer consciously or unconsciously injects the behavior on stage with ritualistic significance, the gesture and the words of the performance, severed now from meaning and significance, open up in the dimension of the absurd (p. 14). Beckett uses the artifice of the stage to plant in the character and in the reader (audience) an experience of defamiliarization and absurdity whose amplification to the rest of life follows inevitably upon this refinement of awareness.

Havel also contends that the "gag defamiliarizes one automatism by another"; it "defamiliarizes the commonly known automatism by the invasion of the truly authentic picture of another commonly known automatism" (pp. 17–18). In Havel's terms Beckett's entire play serves as an extended active second phase. The tramps' boredom, despair, and insecurity at waiting represent the real automatism whose authenticity reasserts itself from time to time, thereby defamiliarizing the subordinate rituals which had momentarily overshadowed it. Havel mentions that the play on convention which is the crux of a film gag defamiliarizes or reveals as absurd our alienation of self without awareness that this is happening. Chaplin's gags implicitly illustrate how the dehumanizing influence of convention alienates the character from his real self. This same comedy, moreover, works on humanizing the spectator by deflating the value of convention.

Beckett's technique differs subtly. When Didi and Gogo step outside their roles to allude directly to the theater, they admit to themselves and remind us of the drama on stage. The mirror/window function is inherent in parody; without it parody ceases to exist. For parody to work one must recognize the original and one's role in it and one must interpret the criticism implied by the distortion. Therefore, recognizing the parody in the play we confess our brotherhood with the tramps. Through parody Beckett mirrors in the audience Didi's and Gogo's recognition and accept- ance of the boundaries of their game-playing and stresses that even at the price of alienation ritual still exists, is indeed vital to give form and content to the void. He likewise deliberately refuses to temper the tramps' ab- surdity through the humanity they share with the audience. If the audience recognizes the human needs and desires simulated on stage, it must also acknowledge the inherent absurdity of the actions consequent upon these needs.

Evocation of the familiar must precede any attempt at defamiliarization. The disarming nature of the familiar is a deceiving disguise for those latent qualities waiting always to spring into life and overcome the usual famil- iarity. Through some strange paradox it is often the most familiar aspects of our lives that suddenly become frighteningly alien. Chaplin manipulates the common, everyday events of life to awaken their comic, often menac- ing potential. He thereby defamiliarizes the quotidian and alienates us to a certain extent from an environment in which we were formerly comfort- able. Chaplin's comedy stems from ritualized behavior which is subse- quently defamiliarized, while Beckett's derives from ritualized language through which he demythifies man's traditions and customs.

Chaplin's tramp, Charlie, wrestles with the mundane realities of life on a physical level—a garbage can, a ladder, a bed, a bear rug, stairs. On a metaphoric level Didi and Gogo involve themselves in an absurdist "com- edy of manners" in which they ridicule the social rituals of a supposedly sophisticated society. Beckett achieves a sense of defamiliarization by giving us glimpses of the familiar and the quotidian in the context of an absurdist drama. The comic potential in Chaplin's films of a banana peel, a wet floor, a broken chair, or an open manhole finds its literary parallel in Beckett's use of conventional speech and habits of thought. In the plays- within-a-play we recognize ourselves, but their place within the larger play defamiliarizes these skits by rendering them absurd. Our habits and rituals are undressed, laid bare, exposed, so to speak, when Beckett demon- strates both their most basic function—to pass the time—as well as their ultimate failure to achieve this satisfactorily. The tightly ordered and structured world of ritual in which the tramps know their cues and their roles is undercut by the aimless and arbitrary universe in which they exist between their skits.

When Didi and Gogo decide to hang themselves "while waiting," we laugh because their logic is absurd. Being dead, neither of them will care whether Godot arrives or not. But when Didi consents to the idea on the grounds that hanging would give them an erection, the defamiliarization works more potently. The absurd intersection in which suicide becomes equated with sexual satisfaction and in which reproduction is made sub-

ject to self-destruction defamiliarizes the banality of all these alternatives
and reasserts the human need for them even while deprecating their
purpose. Beckett makes ingenious existential use of a biological phenomenon. The bridging of these antithetical realities (pain and pleasure, death
and birth) suggests not so much their underlying similarity as their futility
and fruitlessness. While it effects their defamiliarization, the yoking together of the dissimilar conventions also testifies to the tramps' ingenuity
in the face of adversity. It is, thus, man's imaginative ability to survive, to
adapt himself to "given situations" that "makes new" ancient rites (suicide, sex). Ingenuity and imagination defamiliarize the rituals of life, but in
doing so also uncover their origins—man's need for ritual.

Didi and Gogo do not just act out rituals; they literally play with them as
one would play with a toy. Chaplin often showed Charlie at odds with
automatisms such as escalators, cars, barber chairs, and machinery of all
kinds to illustrate the potential absurdity of the mechanism. Beckett's
tramps wind up the automatism and let it play until it peters out; at this
point their sentences often get shorter until finally there is a silence. Ritual
here is much like a wind-up toy that runs smoothly until the spring loses
tension causing the toy to slow down and then to stop altogether. Didi and
Gogo toy with the convention until it has run its course. Simultaneously,
they represent the plaything which we sit watching; they embody our toy.
When they wind down we remember their plight and by extension ours.
The sophisticated conceptual pun of "playing" as in acting out and "playing" as in with a toy unites the parodic humor of the incidents with the
existential anxiety of the dramatic characters.

Didi's and Gogo's behavior assumes mechanical regularity and predict-
ability whenever they enter into ritual. And just when the repetition has
lulled us into complacency, Beckett defamiliarizes it. To provoke both
laughter and reflection, Beckett isolates the convention by first introduc-
ing it seriously; then he filters it through the parody until it emerges in a
form purified of all idiom. One such example occurs when Didi, Gogo, and
Pozzo find themselves caught in the awkwardness of saying good-bye:

ESTRAGON: Then adieu.
POZZO: Adieu.
VLADIMIR: Adieu.
POZZO: Adieu.
             Silence. No one moves.
VLADIMIR: Adieu.
POZZO: Adieu.
ESTRAGON: Adieu.
             Silence.
POZZO: And thank you.
VLADIMIR: Thank *you.*

POZZO:	Not at all.
ESTRAGON:	Yes yes.
POZZO:	No no.
VLADIMIR:	Yes yes.
ESTRAGON:	No no.
	Silence.
POZZO:	I don't seem to be able . . . *(long hesitation)* . . . to depart.
ESTRAGON:	Such is life.

(P. 31v)

Observing all the social niceties, the three suddenly find themselves at a stalemate and, after a silence, Pozzo admits his inability to leave. In the dramatic context of the play his words and our comprehension of them exist on a literal level. Nevertheless, the conventionally figurative sense of Gogo's banal idiom "such is life" (as banal as the French "c'est la vie") clashes in our minds with the literal context on stage. And at precisely that moment when our minds adjust to the pun, the literal action and the literal word meet. Life is, literally, the inability to depart, as the end of each act testifies. Hence, a conventional idiom regains the pragmatic value that takes it out of art (that is, this play-within-a-play and Beckett's drama) and applies it to the lives of the tramps, and by implication to the members of the audience. Convention thus transcends itself.

The fact that the pun is on an idiom is all-important because through it Beckett catches us "in the act" so to speak; he proves how gratefully our minds run on automatic. Once an idiom always an idiom. Gogo explains at one point, "It's so we won't think" (p. 40v). Beckett demonstrates our propensity for avoiding active thought by tricking us into this kind of mental automatism; as Didi says, "What is terrible is to *have* thought" (p. 42r). Our mental habits keep us busy without taking us anywhere. Gogo's "Well? If we gave thanks for our mercies?" (p. 42r) instead of the usual prayerbook "thanks for His mercies" demonstrates a dramatic adjustment from conventional dogma to sardonic cynicism. A deft change of pronoun replaces religious gratitude with existential awareness. Religion is inverted. Man now forgives God His trespasses.

In his manipulation of ritual Beckett subjects the ostensible reality of ritual to its own theatricality in order to uncover the basic permanent reality within. In his discussion of the gag, Havel claims that "[t]he real subject of defamiliarization is . . . the automatism of reality"; and that "[d]efamiliarization extracts reality from the automatism . . ." (p. 16). Defamiliarization, then, extracts reality from reality, meaning that the distilled reality differs markedly from the original one. Havel goes on to say that human activity is dialectical in that powerful emotions striving towards alleviation and equilibrium are centripetal and intensive, while weak emotions seeking to maximize themselves to give an impression that will fulfill a norm of greatness are centrifugal and extensive: "The conflict between the 'small content' and 'great form' . . . is the basis of pathos" (p. 20). The more elaborate Didi's and Gogo's skits become, the more linguistic formulae they incorporate, the more we doubt the sense and worth of these actions and words. In act 1 Pozzo is the actor *par excellence* in the play and therefore also someone whose sentiments are not trustworthy. He cracks his whip to alert everyone to the start of his performance; he frequently uses his vaporizer to clear his voice and repeatedly demands attention from his audience (p. 25r). His puerile, maudlin description of the night sky breaks off suddenly as his real feelings, expressed in his own vernacular emerge briefly: "That's how it is on this bitch of an earth" (p. 26r).

The discrepancy between small content and great form supplies the basis for pathos because it functions to alienate the character involved from himself, and as a result the company of others becomes a necessity. The emotion, being centrifugal, requires constant substantiation. Pozzo must have a slave in order to play the master; he needs an audience to whom to recite: "I don't like talking in a vacuum" (p. 21r). And even when his performance is mediocre he assumes the role of the has-been actor inflated with his own lost dignity: "Gentlemen, you have been . . . civil to me" (p. 26v). Pozzo's hyperbolic behavior defamiliarizes itself even while it alienates Pozzo from himself.

The working of the tramps' pathos is more complex. They defamiliarize one another by each acting the part of the wise fool. In this way Beckett also exposes the particular ritual upon which they draw for comfort and strength:

VLADIMIR: Suppose we repented.
ESTRAGON: Repented what? . . . Our being born?

(P. 9r)

. . . .
VLADIMIR: . . . we have kept our appointment. How many people can boast as much?
ESTRAGON: Billions.

(P. 52r)

In Chaplin's films Charlie's perception or rather misconception of objects defamiliarizes for the audience (but not for Charlie) the conventions which constitute the gag. In *Waiting for Godot* the tramps themselves consciously point to the absurdity of specific conventions and habits. Havel argues that the "gag defamiliarizes something pathetic by something which is not pathetic. . . . The gag [therefore] also depatheticates" (p. 21). The tramps' recognition of their theater depatheticates their playing, saves them from a pathos such as Pozzo's, gives them stature and nobility of the kind Albert Camus lauded in his *Le Mythe de Sisyphe*.

By recognizing their need for and comfort in rituals, Didi and Gogo remain attuned to themselves as limited and imperfect human beings. Pozzo, on the other hand, dehumanizes himself through his self-alienating desire to conform. He obviously believes his performances dignify him, when they in fact only substantiate his need and desire to conform to an external criterion. He therefore feeds that demand which makes him a stranger to himself. Pozzo cannot even satisfy his most pedestrian wants—sitting down for instance—without the aid of a performance involving Gogo (pp. 24v–25r).

Lucky for his part lives on a purely instinctual level, his participation directed solely by self-preservation. Nevertheless, he is absurdly meticulous in his carrier role; as Pozzo explains: "He wants to impress me, so that I'll keep him" (p. 21v). Didi and Gogo wish Godot to "keep" them as well, to save and protect them, and to ensure this they wait: "We have kept our appointment and that's an end to that. We are not saints, but we have kept our appointment" (p. 52r). The repetition of the ambivalent verb "kept" implies that one kind of "keeping" (the tramps') deserves another kind (Godot's).

Havel sees this entire process of the gag as inherently positive because it takes man, the orphan in society, and restores him to himself:

> By defamiliarizing all these "dead" automatisms, by the purposeful ridiculing of everything which seems to be meaningful, by the identification of one's own inappropriateness caused by automatism, man is able to defend himself against self-alienation, recapturing always anew his own identity, returning to himself, to his nature and principle. (P. 24)

What represents the comfort and goal of humanity for a Czech dramatist imprisoned for subversive political activities by a totalitarian government is for Beckett the final frightening and incomprehensible dilemma of existence. That man, despite unwillingness and in defiance of rational awareness, continues to live is both his greatest curse and his most sublime inheritance:

> ESTRAGON: I can't go on like this.
> VLADIMIR: That's what you think.
>
> (P. 61r)

Christopher Innes argues that the progression of Beckett's plays is a "stripping away of worn-out idiom" towards an image of existence refined to the bare essentials: "[T]his vision is quite distinct from that implied by the avant-garde return to myth and ritual with its positive stress on liberating the primitive and rediscovering the 'roots' of human existence" (pp. 209–10). Innes's distinction between Beckett and other modern dramatists touches upon Beckett's view in *Proust* of what can be expected of ritual. The playwright's specific intention is to investigate the "roots" of human existence, in other words, what keeps man planted on this earth, what chains him to life like a "dog to his vomit" (p. 8).

In the play Beckett makes subtle use of this simile to show how man's waste on earth (in literal terms his bodily waste and in figurative terms his waste of time in waiting) obliges him to "stick with it," in other words, to continue living. The prominence of scatology reinforces this connection between waste and man and thereby effectively demythifies man's pretensions. Didi's breath stinks; Gogo, who has trouble urinating, also has smelly feet; Pozzo farts and the tramps imagine fertilizing the ground with their semen. Beckett implies that not for his great achievements in art or intellect does man cling to life, but because he has spewed his by-products about the place; they represent a "signature" of sorts and, once deposited, encumber the donor with a feeling of responsibility and belonging. This insistence on bodily functions not only demythifies man's pretensions to intellect and creativity by pointing to his biological brotherhood with animals, but also offers human equivalents to Beckett's simile of habit and dog's vomit. Indeed, Beckett's canine imagery, among the most sustained in the play, demythifies human superiority by equating man with dogs. Most of the characters in the play are directly or indirectly connected with dogs.

Lucky, ironically christened, is a dog's name and his treatment and appearance are doglike. In act 1 his master, Pozzo, carries a whip and throws him his bones, while Didi and Gogo comment with disgust on his "slobber" and "slaver" and "panting" (p. 18r). In act 2 Lucky plays a Seeing Eye dog to Pozzo's blindman, Didi sings a song about a dog, and Pozzo considers mother earth a "bitch." Even the brothers acting as messengers to Godot mind the sheep and goats in the tradition of dogs. The tramps' "doggedness" most effectively reveals itself in their waiting every evening at the same place for Godot, to whom they insist they are not tied. The loyalty and patience of dogs, most touchingly revealed in their ability to wait inexhaustively for their master—at home, in front of a store—are virtues expounded by men in praise of these pets. All the characters in the play are thus implicated in a dog's life, a connection which in turn elucidates Beckett's ideas regarding habit and its subhuman effects on man.

The power of demythification is consistent throughout the play. Both Christ and God, for instance, are stripped of divinity; Christ's passion is denigrated in contrast to man's suffering: "But where he lived it was warm, it was dry! . . . And they crucified quick" (p. 35r). Godot also seems less than omnipotent. If he really is watching Didi's and Gogo's "playing," he has little reason to appear as this would end his own diversion; his nonappearance effectively provides the momentum for the entire drama. Needing diversion and entertainment and experiencing the same difficulty departing as everyone else, Godot appears as "tied" (p. 15r) as anyone in the play. He seems, therefore, to be made of the same vulnerable stuff as man. The play inverts Pozzo's banal "[M]ade in God's image" (p. 16r) to suggest Godot's share in human frailty, rather than man's share in divinity and godliness. In the universe in which Didi and Gogo exist, man's Christian origins are consistently challenged, suspected, even ridiculed and deflated. In Christ's absence, man must search elsewhere for his prototype. Beckett offers one who is both less dignified, but more appropriate—the wandering tramp character.

Beckett thus makes practical and ironic use of Chaplin's properties and gags to strip his characters of their absurd dignity—to demythify their attempts to pass the time or to make sense of that time. Beckett uses Charlie's derby, his oversized boots, and his propensity for accidents involving his trousers to demythify his characters and, through them, society.

Although all four characters in Beckett's play wear bowlers, the hats' parodic function obliterates the wearers' potential for dignity and respect. Indeed, the hats are singled out as the central comic property in the first of only two classic comedy routines in the entire play (pp. 46v–47r). The second one involves Gogo's trousers. Confusion and futility characterize the hat routine in which, after all the hats are exchanged, Didi keeps Lucky's hat although it is "[n]either more nor less" hideous than his own (p. 47r). In his "performance" Lucky's hat is his thinking cap, so to speak. This implies a connection between man's dignity and his ability to reason or to think. Lucky's performance, however, proving nonsensical and painful, cynically severs this relationship. His thinking causes the others so much pain they forcibly restrain him. Didi, the philosopher in the play, never manages to find a comfortable hat; this suggests that the problem lies not with the hat, but with his head. In act 2 Lucky appears with *"a different hat,"* but is *"burdened as before"* (p. 50r). Clothes do not, therefore, make the man, nor does a hat bestow status or dignity; Lucky is still enslaved.

Juxtaposed to Charlie's sensitive face, small frame, and graceful, swift agility, are the clumsy, oversized boots over which he regularly trips, leading him to embarrassment and trouble. Often in defiance of his best intentions, his feet mercilessly remind him and us of the problem at hand—the escalator, stairs, a manhole, a crack in the ladder rungs.

At the start of the second act Gogo's shoes stand center stage. Beckett's stage instructions insist that they be placed as Chaplin's were in his film signature, *"heels together, toes splayed"* (p. 37v). With his hat man may offer pretensions of gentility, but with his shoes he walks the same dusty road as everyone else. Too small for him, Gogo's boots hurt him and mar his poetic sensibilities; thus man is too big for his shoes, expects too much, and therefore lives with constant disappointment. In Beckett's play Didi's irritating hat suggests the inability of philosophy to elevate man's comprehension of himself and of the world, while Gogo's painful boots metaphorically represent the poet's bumping into life's earthier problems.

In act 1 Didi's and Gogo's suicide attempt is pre-empted by their fears of loneliness. This cancelled suicide, nevertheless, has a human dimension to it, whereas the attempted suicide that ends the play is pitilessly ridiculed with the help of a typical Chaplin gag. At the end of Beckett's play Gogo spends several minutes ignorant that his pants have fallen around his ankles. While at the end of act 1 the absurdity of the tramps' suicide attempt is sensitively tempered by their feelings of friendship for one another, at the end of act 2 nothing mitigates their grotesque and ludicrous actions. The comical incongruity of Gogo standing with his pants around his ankles, innocently asking "Shall we go?", instills a degree of humiliation and indignity that is entirely absent from the first suicide attempt. Beckett implies that failing to kill himself leaves man with his pants down, vulnerable and laughable.

Demythification occurs in degrees as Beckett, through his various parodic devices (the plays-within-a-play, the Chaplinesque characters, the canine imagery, and so on), strips away the automatisms which satirically hide man's essential nakedness, vulnerability, and ridiculousness. By pruning away the layers of ritual in search of the roots keeping man planted to life and to this world, Beckett demonstrates his dramatic intention of exposure, but without any hope of purification. Havel contends that the artist's sense of the absurd (in Beckett this exists as parody) leads to the defamiliarization that achieves the only possible catharsis for contemporary man (p. 24). In Havel's terms as well as in Chaplin's, the exposure of automatism cleanses man of its attraction and influence. But for Beckett human life reveals itself as innately ritualized through routine and automatism. His dramatic focus, therefore, highlights not so much the rites themselves, as the need—innate, incomprehensible, constant—that motivates man and gives meaning to his existence.

Beckett's commentary on Proust, written thirty years before *Waiting for Godot,* helps us to approach his play in the proper spirit of demythification:

> The man with a good memory does not remember anything because he does not forget anything. His memory is uniform, a creature of routine, at once a condition and function of his impeccable habit, an instrument of reference instead of an instrument of discovery. (P. 17)

Beckett warns against allowing the strength of memory to usurp the power of thought, his diagnosis being that remembering is quicker and easier than thinking—is, in fact, automatic. This explains why the characters prefer the comfort and security of the lines and roles learned by rote to the naked insecurity of standing on stage minus a script. Beckett's analogy between the stage and the world and between theater and life forces us to see ourselves and each other as both actor and audience, participant and spectator. This in turn brings up the question of the extent to which we treat life as art. In *Proust* Beckett at one point admonishes:

> Normally we are in the position of the tourist . . . aesthetic experience consists in a series of identifications and . . . Baedeker is the end rather than the means. (P. 11)

The sense of recognition we enjoy tempts us into a false belief in our real familiarity with the world and leads us to the fatal assumption that we therefore know something about our lives.

However, the somnambulistic participation in the mechanical ritual of life is the prerequisite to awakening to a keener, more acute sense of oneself, others, and the existence on earth which unites the two. The acknowledgment of ritual deprived of its epistemological substance does not, however, abolish ritual; rather it transforms an automatic mode of living, in which the person exists metaphorically blind, deaf, and dumb, into a self-conscious, more reflexive one in which the person may choose to "act," but knows at least that he chooses.

To illustrate pointedly and ironically how man usually "thinks," Beckett has Lucky, the mechanical dog, perform:

POZZO: . . . What do you prefer? Shall we have him dance, or sing, or recite, or think, or—
ESTRAGON: Who?
POZZO: Who! You know how to think, you two?
VLADIMIR: He thinks?
POZZO: Certainly. . . . Well, would you like him to think something for us?
ESTRAGON: I'd rather he'd dance, it'd be more fun. . . . Perhaps he could dance first and think afterwards, if it isn't too much to ask him.
VLADIMIR: *(to Pozzo).* Would that be possible?
POZZO: By all means, nothing simpler. It's the *natural order.*
                                              (Pp. 26v–27r. Emphasis mine.)

Pozzo expresses facetious surprise when Gogo's question implies that anyone else in the company can think. Thinking is a performance, like tightrope walking, acted for the pleasure and distraction of the public. Dancing always comes before thinking, just as activity precedes reflexion, automatism anticipates defamiliarization, and ritual looks forward to demythification.

Notes

1. Geneviève Serreau, *Histoire du "nouveau théâtre"* (Paris: Gallimard, 1966), p. 89. (Translation mine.)

2. Samuel Beckett, *Waiting for Godot* (New York: Grove Press, 1954), p. 49v. Subsequent citations from this edition will be noted parenthetically. Each page number is used for both recto and verso sides of a page; hence; "r" is used for recto, "v" for verso.

3. Mircea Eliade, "Myth in the Nineteenth and Twentieth Centuries," in *Dictionary of the History of Ideas* (New York: Charles Scribner's Sons, 1973), 3: 312a.

4. Quoted by Christopher Crocker, "Ritual and the Develoment of Social Structure: Liminality and Inversion," in *The Roots of Ritual,* ed. James D. Shaughnessy (Michigan: William B. Eerdmans, 1973), p. 57.

5. Eliade, 3: 315b.

6. Margaret Mead, "Ritual and Social Crisis," in *The Roots of Ritual,* p. 89.

7. Christopher Innes, *Holy Theatre* (New York: Cambridge University Press, 1981), p. 214. Subsequent citations from this edition will be noted parenthetically.

8. Samuel Beckett, *Proust,* (New York: Grove Press, 1931), p. 8. Subsequent citations from this edition will be noted parenthetically.

9. Václav Havel, "The Anatomy of the Gag," *Modern Drama* 23 (March 1980): 13–24. Subsequent citations from this edition will be noted parenthetically.

The Ritual of Human Techné in *Happy Days*

Phyllis Carey

In nearly all of his works Samuel Beckett has explored the complex relationship between humans and machines. One can readily perceive, for example, the Cartesian body-as-machine motif in *Murphy* and *The Trilogy,* the interplay of human and machine in *Krapp's Last Tape,* and the machine as environment in *The Lost Ones.* In its more subtle manifestations, however, Beckett's treatment of the human vis-à-vis the machine discloses some of its most profound implications. In *Happy Days* Beckett uses ritual to reveal both that which is inherently mechanical in human behavior and that which would prescind the mechanical. Beckett's depiction of Winnie undercuts the human propensity to follow established patterns of behavior, the mechanical rituals of habit. At the same time, *Happy Days* discloses the impotence of ritual as magic—as an attempt to coerce through incantation. In the artistic shaping of the whole, nevertheless, Beckett suggests the potency of aesthetic ritual as an agent of revelation.

Like *Endgame* with its sparse shelter overlooking an exhausted, external world, the very setting of *Happy Days,* with its scorched grass and wasted landscape, suggests the human-machine relationship. In the early versions of *Happy Days,* Beckett made explicit reference to a rocket, which to some degree accounted for the devastation of the play's setting. The omission of the rocket in the final version would seem to have been Beckett's deletion of the concrete in favor of the abstract.[1] What *Happy Days* dramatizes on one level is a world seen from a technological perspective, a mental construct to which humans have continually adapted themselves until they seem to be merely playing out the last stages of a self-destructive ritual.

Superficially, Winnie's rituals disclose the human propensity to adaptation, a mode of standardized, mechanistic behavior, "an automatic adjustment of the human organism to the conditions of its existence."[2] Act 1 underscores the mechanical adaptation inherent in Winnie's rituals. The ringing of the bell, Winnie's clasping her hands, her lips moving in "inaudible player,"[3] her brushing her teeth, polishing her spectacles, sorting

144

through the contents of her bag, unfurling her parasol, listening to the music box are presented as repeated gestures, pseudo-ceremonial acts by which Winnie gets through the day:

> Brush and comb the hair, if it has not been done, or if there is some doubt, trim the nails if they are in need of trimming, these things tide one over. (P. 24)

Winnie's gestures in act 1 are presented as ritualistic, mechanical movements that enable her to avoid confronting the horror of her situation. In her ceremony of severely limited movements, however, one can see the full implications of the human-as-machine metaphor. First, the entropic nature of machines—and therefore of humans, if the metaphor is sustained—is mirrored in Winnie's gestures. Already *"imbedded up to above her waist"* (p. 7) in act 1, Winnie can move only her upper body; in act 2, she can move only her eyes. Beckett uses thermodynamic terms in reference to her gestures in act 1 to disclose the inherent entropy in the human conceived as mechanical system. Winnie puts on her hat and cannot take it off (p. 24); she unfurls her umbrella and cannot close it: "No, something must happen, in the world, take place, some change, I cannot, if I am to move again" (p. 36). What happens, strangely, is the spontaneous combustion of the umbrella, a dramatization—set in fast-forward time-exposure— of entropy: "a measure of the capacity of a system to undergo spontaneous change, thermodynamically specified by the relationship $dS = dQ/T$, where dS is an infinitesimal change in the measure for a system absorbing an infinitesimal quantity of heat dQ at absolute temperature."[4] If the universe is seen as a machine, its entropy necessarily follows; metaphors, in their own internal logic, contain their own determinisms.

The objects Winnie manipulates in act 1 or gazes at in act 2, secondly, become extensions of the human-as-machine metaphor. The toothpaste, lipstick, medicine, and Willie's vaseline are running out; the newspaper is yellow. The conflation of human and object is underscored not only by Winnie's recollections of being inspected like an object by the "last human kind—to stray this way" (pp. 43–44) but also by the equations of humans with animals: the formication joke, which suggests the similarity between humans and ants and the toothbrush bristles, derived from "castrated male swine . . . reared for slaughter" (p. 47), another analogy to the human. The human-as-machine metaphor subsumes all life, including human, into objects to be exploited. As such, the objects lose their distinctiveness as objects, becoming what Martin Heidegger calls *Bestand*, "standing reserve."[5] The orderability and substitutability of objects is stressed, as opposed to their uniqueness and freedom as objects; machines exist to be used, not for their own sake. The contents of Winnie's bag, her gestures, her language, and Winnie herself are all portrayed in *Happy Days* as exploitable and exploited. Human techné, seen primarily in terms of manipulation of objects, is itself subsumed in *Happy Days* by the mechanics of exploitation.

In underscoring the entropy and the exploitation inherent in the human-as-machine metaphor, Winnie's rituals, seen from a mechanistic view-point, disclose the self-destructive nature of the metaphor. That which is automatic in the human becomes externalized into a human construct of the universe and existence itself. The human propensity to standardized patterns and repetitive order, as old as humans themselves,[6] emptied historically of transcendental objectives, is carried in *Happy Days* to its logical—and absurd—conclusion of aimless mechanical adaptation to the system projected. "That is what I find so wonderful. *(Pause.)* The way man adapts himself. *(Pause.)*" (p. 35). What Winnie fails to question but what Beckett's portrayal suggests is that human adaptation, rather than a deter-ministic, automatic adjustment to something beyond human control, might be instead the self-fulfilling accommodation to a human construct, which ultimately betrays a failure in human imagination.

That other visions of human existence are possible is suggested in *Happy Days* both by the incantatory quality of Winnie's ritual of saying and her frequent allusions to literature, and by Beckett's structuring of the ritual of the play to point beyond human words and gestures. It becomes increasingly clear that the action of the play takes place primarily not in Winnie's ever-decreasing gestures but in the interplay of language and silence. Winnie equates saying—consistently with the human-as-machine metaphor—with objects to be manipulated: "Ah yes, so little to say, so little to do, and the fear so great, certain days, of finding oneself . . . left . . . and nothing more to say, nothing more to do" (p. 35). Like the entropy of the objects—human and inanimate in *Happy Days*—"words must fail" (p. 32); they are limited like the objects: "don't squander all your words for the day" (p. 41). Like her polishing and sorting of the contents of her bag, Winnie's saying takes on the form of a repeated ritual—praying her "old prayer" (p. 48), singing her song, telling her story, talking about the objects in her bag. Besides the repeated gestures that help her avoid the "strange-ness" of her situation, Winnie's continual use of verbal clichés and quotes from the past takes on ritualistic overtones.

Winnie's clichés, while manifesting the verbal equivalent of human adaptation—the mechanical application of verbal formulae—also disclose a hermetic approach to reality. Her repeated utterances such as "Another heavenly [or happy] day" (pp. 8, 15, 18, 23, 47, 48, 62, 64) and "wonder-ful" (pp. 10, 11, 12, 141, 18, 20, 24, 31, 35, 36, 39, 41, 58) not only clash ironically with the representational horror of her situation but also become increasingly emptied of meaning by their varied applications and repetition within the play. It is "wonderful" that there is hardly any pain (p. 11) and that "a part remains, of one's classics, to help one through the day" (p. 58). Winnie's repetition of the same words suggests that language—like objects, like the human-as-machine—is being used up in this humanly conceived, entropic universe: "life has taught me that. . . . Yes, life I suppose, there is no other word" (p. 28). Language as mechanical system discloses its inherent limitations. But if Winnie's words, like her gestures, suggest the ongoing transformation (*entropy,* F. Gk. *en,* "in" + Gk. *tropé,* "transformation") of decreasing energy in a mechanical construct of human existence, her more and more desperate need to say and repeat also reveals the human desire to transform sound into meaning, to transmute by will power, as if by alchemy, the inferno of her existence into "another heavenly day" (p. 8). Winnie's ritual of incantation, portrayed as both futile and absurd from the opening line of the play, lays bare both the incantatory qualities inherent in the human desire to impose meaning and the common denominator of the mechanistic and the magical aspects of ritual in human techné.

Jacques Ellul notes: "Our modern worship of technique derives from man's ancestral worship of the mysterious and marvelous character of his own handiwork."[7] Winnie's repeated use of "wonderful," seen from this perspective, takes on additional layers of irony. What once struck humans with awe, elicited primitive worship of the supernatural, and seemingly endowed words with magical, transforming power has evolved full circle, emptying both the human and the words she uses of perhaps one of the most fundamental of human characteristics—wonder.

In the portrayal of the hermetic qualities in Winnie's approach to language, Beckett discloses both what has been lost through human worship of technique and the inadequacy of only the mechanical and the magical in ritual to enable humans to come to terms with techné. That Winnie regards her saying and gestures in hermetic terms is strongly suggested by her inexplicable unwillingness to alter her rituals: "To sing too soon is a great mistake, I find. . . . Do not overdo the bag, Winnie" (p. 32). Similar to the human-as-mechanical-system metaphor, Winnie's words and gestures manifest basic magical techniques that are primarily for defensive and adjustment purposes: "Everything is of a piece, everything is dependent upon everything else; consequently, nothing can be meddled with, nothing modified without threat to the whole structure of beliefs and activities."[8] Winnie's hermetic approach to language discloses the impotency of the metatechnological function of ritual.

Winnie's allusions to her "classics," moreover, reveal the impotency of the mythology that would inform the ritual of her existence. Her omission and distortions and the juxtaposition of her quotes with her ludicrous situation effectively trivialize the humanistic tradition. As Stanley Gontarski notes:

> In Beckett's selection of quotations and oblique references virtually every historical epoch is represented: pre-Christian Greek philosophies, the blind religiosity and Christian idealism of the Middle Ages, Renaissance Humanism, eighteenth-century Rationalism, and nineteenth-century romanticism. The philosophies, literature, and religions of Western man comprise the fragmented mythology against which Winnie fails and suffers, and like a jeweler's foil, mythology highlights the suffering.[9]

Instead of the recognition that the past lives in the present that the ritualistic repetition of the myth is intended to convey, Winnie experiences the radical dichotomy between "the old style" and her present experience. Her quoting of her "classics" becomes a tragicomic and futile attempt to conjure what is patently dead.

In his portrayal of Winnie's failure to exorcise the "strangeness" of her situation through her incantatory repetition, juxtaposed with the human-as-machine metaphor that dominates the visual aspect of the play, Beckett focuses questions that are at the heart of *Happy Days*. Do humans create their own techniques (ritual) or are we—like the robed creatures in Beckett's recent *Quad* I and II—seemingly cogs in a complex system beyond both our understanding and control? *Happy Days* would seem to suggest that the master-victim antinomy—like the Pozzo-Lucky duality in *Godot*—is not only ambiguous but also perhaps misleading. If ritual is seen only as the mechanical adaptation of habit and/or as a defense system to propitiate alien forces, humans and their language are destined to the increasing paralysis of an entropic, impotent mechanical system, victims primarily of their own obsession with mastery. Beckett's structuring of the visual, the language, and the silences, however, discloses in itself another aspect of ritual and of human techné.

Winnie's telling of her story near the end of the play provides the inner myth of the aesthetic ritual in the play. "When all else fails" (p. 54), Winnie repeats the story she has ostensibly told herself many times, the childish story of a small girl's sexual curiosity. The child, undressing her doll under a table in the nursery, is surprised by a mouse, whose "running up her little thigh" symbolizes an assault on sexual innocence. Winnie's cries, merging with those of the character in the story, focus the inner and outer dramas in a moment of horror. While Winnie's rituals suggest eschatological overtones, the story of Milly focuses on origins, the fall from innocence, human vulnerability. Both Winnie and Milly witness to the original sin of having been born.[10]

The inner "myth" of Milly underscores the mythical quality of the play as a whole. The inner "myth" and the outer "myth" coverage in the scream as perhaps the only appropriate verbal response to the human condition—a futile scream, because it is already "too late" (p. 59). Aesthetically, *Happy Days* becomes the ritualistic reenactment of the story of human existence, the repeated ritual of a seemingly eternal torment that is a form of hell.

By gradually emptying words of their significance through repetition, distortion, misapplications, and clichés and by restricting Winnie's movements to her eyes, Beckett focuses the audience's attention more and more on two elements: seeing and silence. What *Happy Days* becomes, aesthetically, it would seem is a ritualistic prelude, designed to prepare the audience for a moment of silent meditation when Winnie and Willie look at each other in the *"Long Pause"* that concludes the play. The question would seem to be not whether Willie is joining Winnie or intends to kill her—as many critics have debated—but rather if the *regard* of these creatures—the one reduced to a quasi-automaton singing the mechanical song of a music box, the other, a pratfalling clown—provides for the audience a recognition scene, a key element not only of classical drama but of ritual as well.

Opposed to the deterministic entropy and impotent attempts at transformation within the play is the aesthetic shaping of the drama itself to provide the viewer a moment of participation in the silence and the stare, an artistic shaping of ritual to enable a transformation of human vision. In *Happy Days,* the dramatic and poetic reveal what reason cannot know, an awakening from the happy "daze" of "our pernicious and incurable optimism"[11]—our mechanical adaptation and our attempts to make reality conform to our wishes—to the horror and the wonder, seemingly dead within us, of being human. In depicting the distortions of human ritual, in deconstructing the metaphors humans have repeatedly reenacted as the real, Beckett shapes his demythologizing as a rite itself to enable its viewing participants to experience once again the rudimentary human emotions that provided the basis for the forming of myths and machines. Human techné stripped of centuries of distortion and exploitation finds its origins in the awe and terror expressed in ritual. To reawaken that awe and terror, Beckett's aesthetic ritual unmakes the metaphors that have become habitual or wishful ways of seeing. Beckett's art, in bringing us to a recognition of the wonder and horror of being human, at the same time reveals to us our primordial techné in the metaphors we shape, which, in turn, shape us.

Notes

1. Stanley Gontarski, *Samuel Beckett's Happy Days: A Manuscript Study* (Columbus: Ohio State University Press, 1977), p. 40.

2. Samuel Beckett, *Proust* (New York: Grove Press, 1931), p. 9.

3. Samuel Beckett, *Happy Days* (New York: Grove Press, 1961), p. 8; hereafter cited parenthetically in the text.

4. *American Heritage Dictionary,* 2d. ed., s.v. "entropy."

5. Martin Heidegger, *The Question Concerning Technology and Other Essays,* trans. William Lovitt (New York: Harper & Row, 1977), p. 17.

6. Lewis Mumford, "Technics and the Nature of Man" in *Technology and Culture: An Anthology,* ed. Melvin Kranzberg and William H. Davenport (New York: Schocken, 1972), p. 204. Mumford, echoing A. N. Hocart, argues here that ritual, along with tool-making, may well have provided the basis for human techné in its standardized patterns and repetitive order.

7. Jacques Ellul, *The Technological Society,* trans. John Wilkinson (New York: Vintage, 1967), p. 24.

8. Ellul, p. 26.

9. Gontarski, p. 73.

10. *Proust,* p. 49.

11. *Proust,* p. 5.

A Blink in the Mirror

From Oedipus to Narcissus and Back in the Drama of
Samuel Beckett

Judith A. Roof

Referring to Clov's inability to sit and his own inability to stand, Hamm proudly but paradoxically states in Samuel Beckett's *Endgame,* "Every man his speciality."[1] The daily struggle of "I can't go on, I'll go on," a struggle against specialization or lack that represents a loss of physical facility through time, takes its course through the history of Hamm's narratives and Nell's memory in *Endgame,* through Winnie's stories in *Happy Days,* and through Vladimir's and Estragon's dim memories of youth in *Waiting for Godot.* Each character in the pairs of characters has indeed become specialized through history. In each play the characters' former wholeness, the subject of renewed revery and thwarted recovery, is translated into the characters' present limitations—Hamm's blindness, Clov's inability to sit, Winnie's entrapment in the mound, Vladimir's bladder problems, and Estragon's problems with his feet. In short, specialization is the result of an historical evolution of lack. The limitations are the recognized result of the passage of time; and thus the recounting of history is the tracing of the image of a formerly total self, while the loss of wholeness through time is poignantly apparent in the image of the other character in the pair who has lost as well, but who retains precisely that which has been lost on the part of the other character. Each character in a pair opposes the other, providing the mirror image not of what is present but of what is no longer present in each.

The mirroring which informs the relationships of the characters in the pairs is a mirror image in so far as it is a reversal, a literal opposition, and in so far as the characters take their cues from the lack(s) evident in the other character. The suggestion of the mirroring of characters in these plays is the suggestion of a narcissism grown sour, of a deadly entrapment of the gaze in a now-stagnant pool. However, what appears to be a narcissistic structure is not; the dynamic between these paired characters is not so much one of an opposition or of an irresistible attraction, but of a filling in, of a supplementariness, a "specialization," which forces the

151

constant redefinition of self in terms of the past and in terms of the other. The pairs interact in a dialectical dynamic, from present to past, from one to the other, in an alternation which is ultimately an evocation of an oedipal search for identity through the morass of an endless history.

Genuine narcissism, in the form of a libidinous investment in the mind's own eye, appears paradoxically to emerge when Beckett changes from pairs of characters to triangles in *Play* (1963), in *Come and Go* (1968), and later in *Catastrophe* (1982). Abandoning pairs, Beckett peoples these plays with triads—M, W1, and W2 in *Play,* Flo, V, and Ru in *Come and Go,* and the Director, Assistant Director, and Protagonist in *Catastrophe*. What appears to be the suggestion of an oedipal triangle in these plays shifts from a completely oedipal revision of the past in *Play* and *Come and Go* or of the stage in *Catastrophe* to a narcissistic gaze into self within the oedipal which reflects the opposition and specularity of the relationship between the audience and the stage. The shift from the oedipal to a narcissism enabled by the oedipal in the corpus of Beckett's drama is an alternation which not only moves from dyads to triads in individual plays, but which works within the plays themselves as an alternation between the oedipal search for identity and the deadly rest of the narcissistic gaze. In this context, moving from the oedipal to the narcissistic is not a regression, nor is the subsequent return to the oedipal stage a maturation; the drama is simply an alternation from one to the other, analogous to the alternation from A to B to A in *Act Without Words II.*

What is oedipal and what is narcissistic in Beckett's drama is defined by the characters' ability to perceive the totality of themselves in their images reflected in the other as well as by their ability to keep such recollection within the spectacle, within language, and within their interaction with other characters. Not a question of plot or conflict, the oedipal refers primarily to the question of one's identity and relation to others as that devolves on stage. In relation to this mirror of the stage and the mirrored characters, the oedipal is the expression of the symbolic perception of totality which is inaugurated by the stage in development Lacan names the "Mirror Stage." The narcissistic is, then, the gaze at self in the mirror, an act only understood after a perception of totality, in other words, historically. In this way the oedipal enables a perception of the narcissistic which precedes it chronologically.

In "The Mirror Stage" Lacan calls the episode of the child gazing at his/her image in the mirror "a drama."[2] For Lacan the mirror stage is the point at which the child, still immobile, recognizes via the total image of him or herself in the mirror the idea of a totality of body and self not yet acquired. As Lacan states:

> The mirror stage is a drama whose internal thrust is precipitated from insufficiency to anticipation—and which manufactures for the subject,

caught up in the lure of spatial identification, the succession of fantasies that extends from a fragmented body-image to a form of its totality that I shall call orthopaedic—and, lastly, to the assumption of the armour of an alienating identity, which will mark with its rigid structure the subject's entire mental development.[3]

As a drama, the process described by Lacan proceeds from "insufficiency to anticipation," from "the image of the body in bits and pieces" to an image of totality. At the same time, the process proceeds in the opposite direction toward a retroactive recognition of a past fragmentation which is comprehended only once the child perceives the image as total. The mirror stage thus appears to be the opposite of the history of Beckett's characters, who in a present fragmented state remember a totality.

The impetus of the mirror stage, then, is the action of recognizing both the wholeness of the image projected into the mirror and the fragmentation from which one has just escaped: it is a drama of a placement within history, through which both knowledge and wholeness become relative. The drama is a point of transition from timelessness into time, from present to future to a recognition of past as past made by means of visual perception. As Lacan later writes: "What realizes itself in my history, is not the past definite of what was since it is no longer, nor even the present perfect of what has been in what I am, but the future anterior of what I will have been for what I am in the process of becoming."[4] Because what is perceived, like a drama, is an illusion, the mirror stage is always a misperception, a misrecognition which nonetheless leads to a greater understanding and a greater terror. The mirror stage is the tragedy of perpetual loss, of the acquisition of a rigid "armour," of an entry into the anxiety of history as well as a moment of jubilation and "self-mastery."

The illusion of unity the child perceives in the mirror, in which a human being is always looking forward to self-mastery, entails a constant danger of sliding back again into the chaos from which he or she started. "It hangs over the abyss of a dizzy Ascent in which one can perhaps see the very essence of anxiety."[5] This anxiety is comparative, the result of seeing a past during which self-mastery was missing, but it is also the foundation of an oedipal question of relation and identity. The mirror stage is "an identification" with an image of totality, a moment which commences the child's relation to the image in the mirror as an image of an other, a relation which enables the oedipus complex.

While thrusting the child into a kind of knowledge which forces him or her into an oedipal search for identity and relation to others, the mirror stage also enables narcissism, since the image of self is first comprehended at the mirror stage.[6] This "primary narcissism" is in dynamic opposition with the sexual libidinous investment represented by the oedipal conflict. The libidinal investment in self at the moment of the mirror stage, while making possible the oedipal, also provides the tension

between the two libidos, tension Lacan connects to the "existential nega-
tivity" grasped "only within the limits of self-sufficiency of consciousness."[7] In drama, as in the mirror stage, the oedipal comprehends
both an oedipal, sexual libido and a narcissistic libido. The difference
between them lies in the direction of the gaze of the character: in the
oedipal the gaze is directed toward another person, place, or time; in the
narcissistic, the character's gaze is directed to or returned to self.

The connections among the drama of the mirror stage, the oedipus
complex, and the notion of the centrality of an oedipal search for identity
in theater as suggested by Francis Fergusson and André Green is the
relationship among the ability to perceive totality acquired at the mirror
stage (the initial ability to form and relate to an image and an access to the
symbolic), the specific content of the later Oedipus complex, and the
repetition and reflection in theater of both this ability to identify and an
oedipal content open to the gaze of the audience. Fergusson makes the
connection between theater and the story of Oedipus: "*Oedipux Rex* is a
crucial instance of drama, if not *the* play which best exemplifies this art in
its essential nature and completeness."[8] *Oedipus Rex* is an instance of the
question of an identity dependent upon the unraveling of history and a
gradual enlightenment open to the gaze of the audience. Like the mirror
stage, the perception of the image, or of identity, changes the act of
perception forever. "The object, indeed, the final perception, the 'truth,'
looks so different at the end from what it did at the beginning that
Oedipus's action itself may seem not a quest, but its opposite, a flight."[9]
Like a child at the mirror stage, Oedipus moves toward a mastery of self at
the same time that he apprehends the horror of a chaos which underlies
that mastery.

The structure of the drama itself is reliant upon the tensions of the
mirror stage. Like the mirror stage, "the theatre has its effect only insofar
as its ways are misunderstood by the spectators."[10] What is thought to be
seen on stage is not what is seen; it is mis-taken. The watching of a play,
like the gaze into the mirror "seems to drive the action outside of itself"
by the very fact of the gaze or participation in the image.[11] A "recognition
by representation," theater, like the mirror stage, proceeds from an "igno-
rance to knowledge—whether on the part of the hero or the spectator."[12]
This (mis)recognition of what appears to be other, outside, as alienated is a
resituation vis-à-vis the other in the image and in relation to what was that
is no longer and what is that will soon no longer be.

In the work of Samuel Beckett, the relationship of the characters to the
recognition mentioned by both Fergusson and Green seems to be re-
versed. Wholeness is retroactive and historical instead of fragmentation.
The characters perceive their fragmentation in relation to a past wholeness instead of perceiving a past fragmentation in a present image of

totality. Hamm posits an ironically positive proof that there is nature: "But we breathe, we change! We lose our hair, our teeth! Our bloom! Our ideals!" (p. 11). As they are drawn back again and again to the question of former wholeness, Clov exclaims, "We too were bonny—once. It's a rare thing not to have been bonny—once." (p. 42).

The dyadic plays, if a term may be coined for those plays in which pairs of characters interact as opposites, represent a primarily oedipal struggle in terms of history and the Other, centered around an anxiety about fragmentation and placement in history. The struggle to make time pass, to make waiting go more quickly, to fill up time is a struggle to regain the mastery and jubilation of the first glance in the mirror. Mastery for each character is always a memory recaptured fleetingly through Hamm's chronicles, Nagg's jokes, Winnie's stories, and Lucky's lecture. Jubilation, while sometimes past as in Nell's memories of Lake Como, is also projected into the future as a kind of grim jubilation when Godot comes, or night falls, or Winnie can play her music, or when Clov evokes his dream of a "world where all would be silent and still and each thing in its last place, under the last dust" (p. 57).

The struggle to determine placement in space and time and identity in relation to one another is an oedipal struggle which takes place entirely in terms of the other character(s). Though there is some specifically oedipal content in Hamm's battles with his "accursed progenitor" Nagg, or Vladimir's and Estragon's expectations from the ever-potential Godot, and in Winnie's relationship to Willie, the oedipal mode of these plays is a search for a placement in a history perpetually out of control, as evidenced by the constant lack in self as reflected in the presence in/of the other character. The mirrored characters reflect one another by responding to and by reassuring one another that they are no longer what they were and not yet what they are to be. Vladimir and Estragon fear to leave one another, yet constantly toy with the idea of parting, as do Hamm and Clov. Winnie fears that Willie will not appear from his hole. They remember each other's past, when Winnie wasn't trapped, when they were young on bicycles in the Ardennes, when there was plenty, when there was love.

The struggle to revise, refine the reality of a former illusion of totality in terms of the mirror Other is the impossibility that compels the visions of darkness and emptiness that stand as tempting mirages of peace when all time, and hence all history and struggle, cease. Thus, the ending of a "day," of each long gaze, is crucial. In *Waiting for Godot* Vladimir and Estragon are left standing as night falls. Though they express a desire to go, they do not move. Though they indicate at the beginning of the second act that they have spent the night apart, night is no time of peace or relief. Estragon is beaten and Vladimir struggles with his bladder. Their static search for Godot is either unrelieved by the break in the gaze afforded by darkness, or darkness cannot finally loose them from the image of chaos that awaits each moment if Godot does not come. Although Hamm's blindness does not represent the insight of Oedipus, neither does not-seeing disable the function of the mirror. Darkness is no answer and Vladimir and Estragon are doomed to repeat, almost, the ritual of the daily mirror.

In *Endgame,* Clov's ending gaze at Hamm, who has escaped behind the veil of the stancher, is no escape or ending either. The gaze in the play is always Clov's—he is the locator in space. Hamm's blindness is the presence of vision in Clov, which Clov can see in its reflection as lack in Hamm. The final image of the play is not the vision of empty peace of which Clov has dreamed; rather, it is prototypical of the continuing mirror relationship of Hamm and Clov, with Clov surveying his own desire to escape in Hamm's unconsciousness—an unconsciousness which nonetheless provokes dreams that remind them both of their own missing parts and of amputation of the world.

Happy Days shifts from the apparently narcissistic self-involvement which ends the first act to the frightening engagement of the gaze at the end of the second act. At the end of act 1 Willie reads aloud from the newspaper ironical references to himself—"Opening for smart youth," "Wanted bright boy."[13] Winnie regards herself in prayer: "Pray your old prayer, Winnie" (p. 48). Both characters gaze into a narcissistic mirror—the newspaper, god—which is outside the duo. What appears to be narcissistic is in fact oedipal; both characters speak their desire, an element of socialization. At the end of act 2, they gaze at one another at last, succeeding in social contact, but in fact experiencing a narcissistic moment of grim identity, a misunderstood image of complementary totality. Willie, who is mobile, can provide the look he has often kept from Winnie. Winnie can now return the gaze, finding her "happy day," but seeing in Willie's reduced mobility her own entrapment. The gaze at the end of the second act of *Happy Days* provides assurance, albeit somewhat questionable assurance in presence, even if such presence is the presence of a lack. It also simultaneously provokes a doubt and a fear as Winnie, *"Smile off,"* and Willie gaze at one another in the endless trap of a mirror.

Though the characters in these earlier dyadic plays mirror one another and see themselves in one another in a way similar to the image the child sees in the mirror in the mirror stage, the characters are not fixed on an image of themselves in any kind of narcissistic gaze. They are fixed, rather, on the lack in self reflected by the other, since there is no escape from history or from each other in any of the plays. Paradoxically, the triadic plays, those with three central characters, superficially seem to be oedipal struggles as well; however, the characters in each of these plays appear to find a false resolution in narcissism, a narcissism which becomes merely a

part of the overarching alternation between the oedipal and the narcissistic within the oedipal.

The first gaze of the mirror stage founds narcissism as well as the
oedipal conflict. As Freud says in his essay "On Narcissism: An Introduction," narcissism is a self-criticism of conscience based on self-observa-
tion. Seeking themselves as love objects, the narcissistic characters
engage in a kind of self-preservative activity which leads the gaze inside to
self instead of outside to the world. Narcissism is, thus, "the libidinal
complement to the egoism of the instinct of self-preservation."[14] As the
other half of the dialectic observed by Lacan between a narcissistic
investment in an image of self and the oedipal sexual investment in the
image of the Other, the narcissistic gaze appears to stop history, to stop
time, and to prevent questions of placement and the anxiety of falling back
into chaos. Narcissism is, however, also a paralyzing illusion of joinder
with self as Other rather than a jubilant image of totality.

Play, Come and Go, and *Catastrophe* all end in a narcissistic gaze
which appears to come as an answer to or relief from the oedipal, but
which is really simply the second stage in an alternation between the
oedipal and the narcissistic. What is at stake in this alternation is finally
only different ways of gazing into that mirror of theater and self which
promises, but which may never deliver, that mastery which it seems to
promise. In *Play,* the situation narrated by the three characters, M, W1,
and W2, in response to the probing light is decidedly oedipal. *Play* consists of two repetitions of a two-part recital by three characters who
appear as heads emerging from urns. As the light shines, apparently
randomly, on each of them, they recite their respective parts in a past love
triangle which existed among the three. Each can only tell when the light
shines on him or her. The story proceeds, moving from three separate
points of view in three totally nonresponsive monologues. In the middle of
the play, the narratives shift from a concern for the past to an obsessive
and narcissistic preoccupation with the light and with self. The play then
repeats, shifting from the narcissistic to the oedipal again.

That the first part of *Play* is oedipal both in content and in the direction
of the gaze is, of course, obvious from the storyline. The characters are in
history, though situated in an uncertain spot after the events they narrate.
Their monologues do not evoke or reproduce the situation, nor do the
characters attempt, as did Hamm and Clov or Vladimir and Estragon, to
situate themselves within a history. Still, their gaze is fixed at a point
outside of themselves, at the other characters in the triangle. The fact that
the narratives are distinctly past tense brings into question their motivation in retelling the story, a motivation objectively situated in the movement of the light "prod" which appears to force them to tell. The
characters are not working out the oedipal knot which underlies the

triangle. M, in fact, clings tenaciously to his fantasy of having both women, mother and other women, as if he had never passed through the threat of castration at all. The two women both desire M in competition with one another in an oedipal struggle. Instead of being a cathartic process, the retelling of the love triangle serves as an impetus for somewhat regressive and illusory self-preservative instincts, for a fixation on self in relation to the insistent shining of the light in hopes that a fixation on the history and fragmentation of the self will stop, will return to the oedipal illusion of mastery of the narrative or to silence and nonexistence or nonawareness of self.

The second half of the play is the drama of relation to the image of self as reflected in and by the light. The characters all react to the light, wishing to revel or play in it as does M, or wishing to hide from it in darkness as do the women. For M the light enables fantasy as well as forcing a vision of self. As he continues his fantasy of the two women in a dinghy on a summer's afternoon (a fantasy finally of an intense fixation on self as the object of desire), he becomes aware of the agency of the light that forces him to see self. He says, "Have I lost . . . the thing you want? Why go out? Who go—;"[15] and later "Why not keep glaring at me without ceasing? I might start to rave and—*(hiccup)*—bring it up for you" (p. 58). At the end of the second part, M is completely aware of the mechanism of the light but not aware of his own narcissism: "Looking for something. In my face. Some truth. In my eyes. Not even;" and he continues, "Mere eye. No mind. Opening and shutting on me. Am I as much—*Spot off M. Blackout. Three seconds. Spot on M.* Am I as much as . . . being seen?" (p. 61). M's engagement with his own fantasy, unrecognized by him as a narcissistic involvement with self, becomes evident in his interaction with the light: he sees it in his final question of the light concerning himself as the object for his own gaze projected onto the light as the light is projected onto him.

The response of the two women to the light is less happily narcissistic, perhaps ironically, since Freud credits women with a greater self-contentment and a desire to be the objects of admiration rather than the admirers.[16] While M delights in the attentions of the two, the women are both anxious for the light to leave them. W1, who continues her jealousy through visions of the other two together, desires darkness: "Silence and darkness were all I craved. Well, I get a certain amount of both. They being one" (p. 59). She later demands of the light, "Weary of playing with me. Get off me. Yes" (p. 60). Her projection onto the light of her own desire for darkness is the desire for an escape from the self of the mirror and of history.

W2 responds to the gaze of the light by perceiving herself as crazy, "A shade gone. In the head. Just a shade. I doubt it" (p. 60). She sees in the light, and thus in herself, her own disjuncture, her own inability to escape.

Earlier, she asks herself, "What do you do when you go out? Sift?" (p. 57); and she describes the effort of the gaze, "like dragging a great roller, on a scorching day. The strain . . . to get it moving, momentum coming—*Spot off W2. Blackout. Three seconds. Spot on W2.* Kill it and strain again" (p. 57). The weariness of self evident in her unsuccessful attempt to characterize herself as insane is the same weariness as that of W1. The fixation on self through the agency of the light is no happier gaze than the earlier (and later) oedipal gaze to the past. The alternation in *Play* between the oedipal and the narcissistic provides finally no relief from the gaze of the eye of self as manifested in the agency of the light. M's final recognition of the gaze itself is a question that shifts him back into his almost voyeuristic oedipal recounting of the original triangle. For M, both oedipal and narcissistic come to the same fantasy of play and escape in play. As he says in the second half, "I know now, all that was just . . . play. And all this? When will all this—;" and later "When will all this have been . . . just play?" (p. 54)

The characters in *Play* are always in flux, from others to self, from self to a problematic conflict with others. The gaze in *Play* is deconstructed; the mind's eye, the mere eye, the light which projects from outside their own narcissistic concentrations is the same narcissistic light which promotes the oedipal affair. As it shifts from one to the other, so the characters shift from light to darkness, from history to self and back. The progress of *Play* is rather like that of Sisyphus, a struggle rather than a progression, leading only to the brief blink of silent solace as the light shifts from one to the other.

In *Come and Go* the number of alternations between the oedipal and the narcissistic is increased in a sort of denial and embrace of the narcissistic in the oedipal. The question of the gaze among the three characters, Vi, Flo, and Ru, is a question about and simultaneous denial of knowledge and history. In *Come and Go,* the three women participate in a circular ritual of absence and knowledge. As the three sit together on a bench, the character in the middle leaves, one of the remaining women slides over to fill in the gap, and the two speak together about whether the absent character has changed, how she looks, and whether or not she knows. The two gaze at one another, express the sentiment that they hope the absent character does not know, and the absent character returns to their silence. This occurs three times and, at the end of the play, the three speak briefly about the past and then join hands in an interlocking circle.

When the three are together on stage, the process is an oedipal quest for placement in history and an acknowledgement and denial of change. In the first cycle of the ritual, as Vi has left, Flo asks Ru what she thinks of Vi. As Ru answers that she sees "little change," Flo moves to the center and whispers in Ru's ear. Ru's response is to ask whether or not Vi realizes and

Flo responds, "God grant not."[17] During the exchange about knowledge, the stage directions explicitly state that the characters "look at each other" (p. 67). The process is repeated three times, with the questions of appearance and knowledge ending in a mirrored denial of the absent character's knowledge as the women on stage gaze into each other's eyes.

The memory of a past relationship "in the playground at Miss Wade's" (p. 67), which emerges when the three are together, is cut off, silenced by the almost narcissistic inquiry into the appearance of the others. The questions about appearance: "What do you think of Vi?" (p. 67), "How do you find Flo?" (p. 68), and "How do you think Ru is looking?" (p. 68), are questions about an image or appearance that evokes a question about placement in time. That the question about appearance is asked during the absence of the character begins a shift to a narcissistic silence, which ends with the mirrored glance between the two characters and a denial of knowledge or a denial of the "truth" of the appearance: "God grant not" (p. 67), "God forbid" (p. 68), "Please God not" (p. 68). The evocation of the name of the father at the end of each interchange between the two reintroduces the absent character and recommences the oedipal-to-narcissistic cycle.

Although we do not know what is said in the whispered exchanges between the pairs of characters on stage, their reactions to it are extreme. The whispers are near silences, like the silence begged for by Ru in the first interchange, "Let us not speak" (p. 67). The lapse into silence is the beginning of a shift away from an oedipal or potentially oedipal interchange where they might be forced to place themselves in time and history. The departure of one character visibly shifts the stage from an oedipal three to a narcissistic two. The whispers signal the final shift from language and knowledge to a mirrored gaze which dissolves back into the oedipal at the simultaneous denial of knowledge and evocation of God.

At the end of the play, the three place themselves in a kind of memory after Vi's query, "May we not speak of the old days? *(Silence)* Of what came after? *(Silence)* Shall we hold hands in the old way?" (pp. 68–69). Though her questions remain unanswered, the three hold hands, presumably in "the old way," by interconnecting all of their hands in what becomes the equivalent of a circle. They present a unified and completely joined front, facing the audience. Joining their images in a simultaneous recognition and denial of history, they become the mirror. The knowledge and placement in the history of the mirror stage reverts to a joinder with the narcissistic mirrors of one another that both denies the image of totality perceived during the mirror stage by denying knowledge and history and presents a final image of totality as a mirror to the audience in the theatre. Flo's final words, "I can feel the rings" (p. 69), complete the binding cycles of their alternation from oedipal to narcissistic. Their identity is joint and shared; they face off against an audience who may or may not "know."

The act of facing off against or mirroring the audience also occurs in Beckett's more recent play, *Catastrophe*. In *Catastrophe,* three characters, the Director, the female Assistant, and the Protagonist, are blocking a theatrical spectacle referred to by the Director as "our catastrophe."[18] Luke is "in charge of lighting off-stage," but, like the light in *Play,* his role is crucial in making seen what is to be seen. The main action of *Catastrophe* is a stripping action in which the darkly clothed protagonist who is standing on a plinth is gradually stripped of masking clothes. The stripping is accomplished at the orders of the director, who has a passion for revealing every detail of the protagonist's body and whitening all of the surfaces. The female assistant has previously arranged the protagonist as black and completely covered. While the female wants the protagonist all black, the Director calls for light, both for his cigar which is constantly going out and for the spectacle of the Protagonist on stage. The Director objects to the Assistant's desire for what he calls "explicitation," denying the Protagonist a gag and the raising of his head.

The struggle in the first part of *Catastrophe* is an oedipal struggle for possession of the image of the protagonist. Both the Director and the Assistant Director make the Protagonist in their own rather grimly narcissistic image, yet struggle with one another for the right to possess that image. The Director as father, who carries and must have a lit cigar, unmasks the image created by the Assistant Director by stripping away the layers of clothing to reveal underneath his own aging hands with "fibrous degeneration" (p. 298), his own shivering recognized by the Assistant, his own moulting hair. Unmasked by this father and mother, the Protagonist doesn't utter even "a squeak" (p. 299).

Taken over by the father, the Protagonist is now subject to the light which the Director directs should shine only on his bowed head. In the battle between the darkness desired by the Assistant and the light demanded by the Director, the Protagonist has the last word. While the Director leaves the stage masked by forbidding the Protagonist to raise his head, the Protagonist does raise his head and "fixes on the audience" (p. 301). The oedipal struggle to create a theater has resulted in a theater of a narcissistic mirror which, like the end of *Come and Go,* fixes on the audience. The long gaze that outlasts the "distant storm of applause" which occurs when the light comes up on his bowed head is a mirror which has previously been the site of the oedipal struggles of the Director and the Assistant Director. In *Catastrophe* the making of theater itself has been the shift from the oedipal to the narcissistic, from the spectacle of an oedipal fight over a narcissistic image on stage to the narcissism of the gaze which mirrors the audience. Raising his head is a final stripping of the mask of theater itself, the final revelation that makes the applause stop and brings to the fore a fear of the mirror, which is perhaps ultimately the reflection of Luke, the "light," as it forces an image of the self gazing at the self.

The metatheatrical quality of *Catastrophe* connects the alternation between the oedipal and the narcissistic to the process of theater itself. A question which revolves around the ability to perceive an image which is inaugurated during the mirror stage, the question of the gaze in theater is in Beckett the question of a shift from an oedipal search for identity in time and space to a search for self-knowledge in the gaze at self. However, the narcissism which appears in *Play* becomes a narcissism that is connected to the relationship between audience and stage. The characters in *Play* face self as they face the light, which is coincidentally the only means by which they are seen at all. Being seen means being seen by an audience and the audience is the audience of self. In the same way, what the audience sees about itself occurs as it participates not only in the oedipal struggles of the characters it watches, like Luke in *Catastrophe,* off-stage, but also in the gaze straight at itself made by the characters in *Come and Go* and by the Protagonist.

Watching theater is gazing into the mirror, placing oneself between history and chaos. The alternation between oedipal and narcissistic is the essence of this mirror that enables and relies upon both. That Beckett's drama alternates this dynamic both within individual plays and within his work as a whole replicates this essential relationship between self and theater, between audience and stage, between self and history, and between the experience of the audience and the search for identity afforded by the theater. Like Oedipus, we are thrust into a history from whence come both chaos and identity; like Narcissus, we gaze at the deadly pool whose only answers can be our own. We can feel the rings.

Notes

1. Samuel Beckett, *Endgame* (New York: Grove Press, 1984), p. 10. All subsequent references are to this edition.
2. Jacques Lacan, *Ecrits: A Selection,* trans. Alan Sheridan (New York: Norton, 1977), p. 4.
3. Ibid., p. 4.
4. Ibid., p. 86.
5. Jacques Lacan, "Some Reflections on the Ego," *International Journal of Psychoanalysis* 34 (1953): 15.
6. Jane Gallop, *Reading Lacan* (Ithaca, N. Y.: Cornell University Press, 1985), p. 121.
7. Lacan, *Ecrits,* p. 6.
8. Francis Fergusson, *The Idea of a Theater* (Princeton: Princeton University Press, 1949), p. 13.
9. Ibid., p. 17.

10. André Green, *The Tragic Effect,* trans. Alan Sheridan (New York: Norton, 1979), p. 6.

11. Ibid., p. 7.

12. Ibid., p. 18.

13. Samuel Beckett, *Happy Days* (New York: Grove Press, 1961), p. 48. All subsequent references are to this edition.

14. Sigmund Freud, "On Narcissism: An Introduction," *The Standard Edition of the Complete Psychological Works,* trans. James Strachey (London: Hogarth, 1953–74), 14:74.

15. Samuel Beckett, *Play,* in *Cascando and Other short Dramatic Pieces* (New York: Grove Press, 1964), pp. 43–66. All subsequent references are to this edition.

16. Freud, p. 69.

17. Samuel Beckett, *Come and Go,* in *Cascando and Other Short Dramatic Pieces* (New York: Grove Press, 1964), pp. 67–71. All subsequent references are to this edition.

18. Samuel Beckett, *Catastrophe,* in *The Collected Shorter Plays of Samuel Beckett* (New York: Grove Press, 1984), pp. 295–301. All subsequent references are to this edition.

Contributors

Susan D. Brienza received her Ph.D. in English from the University of Pennsylvania in 1976 and is an Assistant Professor of English at the University of California, Los Angeles. She has received several grants to study Beckett manuscripts, has published on Beckett in *ELH* (1976), *Journal of Modern Literature* (1977), *Modern Language Notes* (1980), and *Journal of Beckett Studies* (Fall 1982). Her book *Samuel Beckett's New Worlds: Style in Metafiction* (1987) treats the late prose. She has spoken on Beckett at several meetings and was one of the original panelists at the MLA meeting out of which this book has grown.

Katherine H. Burkman, editor, received her Ph.D. in theater from Ohio State University in 1968 and is a Professor of English at Ohio State University. She has been concerned with ritual in modern drama in her two books, *The Dramatic World of Harold Pinter: Its Basis in Ritual* (1971) and *The Arrival of Godot: Ritual Patterns in Modern Drama* (1986), and has published several articles on modern drama. She has written on Beckett for *Arizona Quarterly* (1983) and *Papers in Comparative Literature* (1984) and has spoken on him at several meetings.

Phyllis Carey received her Ph.D. from Marquette University, Milwaukee, Wisconsin, in 1984 and is currently an Assistant Professor of English there. Her paper, "Beckett's Pim and Joyce's Shem," was presented at the IX Annual International James Joyce Symposium in Frankfurt, Germany, and is forthcoming in the *James Joyce Quarterly*. She presented "The Making of Ritual in *Quad* I and II" at a Beckett conference in Stirling, Scotland in 1986, and her manuscript "Language in Technocracy: Samuel Beckett and the Word" is currently being considered for publication.

Claudia Clausius is writing her doctoral thesis on the concepts of time and memory in the dramas of Harold Pinter. She taught twentieth-century literature at the University of Toronto for several years, after which she held the position of English Don at Trinity College for two years. She lectures as part of the PACE program (Public Affairs and Continuing Education) in conjunction with the Shaw and Stratford festivals, has published articles in *Status of Women News* and *Canadian Woman Stud-*

ies, and has given a number of papers at major conferences. Her book on comic theory in Charles Chaplin's films is forthcoming.

MARY A. DOLL received her Ph.D. from Syracuse University in 1980 and is currently with the University of Redlands English Department in California and the Whitehead Center there. She has presented papers on ritual, dream, and myth at national conferences, and her articles on Beckett have appeared in *The Journal of Beckett Studies* and *The Journal of Mental Imagery.* She is currently working on a book on Beckett and myth.

MARTHA FEHSENFELD is an actress and scholar who has done extensive work on Samuel Beckett. She has played the role of Winnie in *Happy Days,* touring in North Carolina and Georgia, and at La MaMa Theatre, ETC, New York City, in 1983. She also attended and recorded the rehearsals of the Beckett/Whitelaw production of *Happy Days* in London in 1979. She has published articles on Beckett in *Modern Drama* and *Theatre Journal* as well as reviewing for *World Literature Today.* She is co-author of *Beckett in the Theatre* for John Calder Publishers and is the designated editor for *The Letters of Samuel Beckett* for Grove Press.

ROSETTE C. LAMONT teaches at the Graduate Center of the City University of New York in the French Ph.D. Program and at Queens College. She has edited and contributed to *Ionesco: A Collection of Critical Essays* and *The Two Faces of Ionesco,* has written many articles on modern French drama, among which are "La Farce Metaphysique de Samuel Beckett," in *Samuel Beckett, Configuration Critique* 8 (1964), "Krapp, un Anti-Proust," in *Cahiers de l'Herne,* ed. Tom Bishop, and "Beckett's Metaphysics of Choiceless Awareness" in *Samuel Beckett Now,* ed. Melvin J. Friedman (1970). Professor Lamont has often spoken on Beckett at meetings and was granted the honor of being elected to the rank of officer in the French Order of Arts and Letters.

SUSAN MAUGHLIN is an artist who is also presently a graduate student in English at Ohio State University.

LOIS MORE OVERBECK, who received her Ph.D. in 1979 from the University of Pennsylvania, is Assistant Professor of English at Spelman College, Atlanta. She has studied Beckett manuscripts at Ohio State University, Washington University, and in England under grants from the National Endowment for the Humanities. She has published articles in *Drama Conference Papers* (University of Florida) and in the Modern Language Association's *Approaches to Teaching Ibsen's "A Doll House."* She is editor of The Beckett Circle, has presented many papers on Beckett's dramaturgy, and was one of the original panelists at the MLA meeting out of which this book has grown.

JUDITH A. ROOF received her Ph.D. from Ohio State University in 1984 and is an Assistant Professor of English at Illinois State University in Normal, Illinois. She has published in *Helicon* (1982), has presented papers on Beckett at several meetings, and is Associate Editor of *Literature and Psychology*.

STEPHEN WATT received his Ph.D. in English from the University of Illinois-Urbana in 1982. An Assistant Professor of English at Indiana University, he was one of the speakers on ritual in Beckett's plays at the 1984 MLA meeting out of which this book has grown. He has published articles in *The Journal of Irish Literature* (1985), *Comparative Drama* (1985), *Mosaic* (1984), *Eire-Ireland* (1983), and *Studies in Iconography* (1980).

Index

167